It is clear that the decline of a language must ultimately have political and economic causes: it is not due simply to the bad influence of this or that individual writer. But an effect can become a cause, reinforcing the original cause and producing the same effect in an intensified form, and so on indefinitely. A man may take to drink because he feels himself to be a failure, and then fail all the more completely because he drinks. It is rather the same thing that is happening to the English language. It becomes ugly and inaccurate because our thoughts are foolish, but the slovenliness of our language makes it easier for us to have foolish thoughts.

George Orwell, *Politics and the English Language*

Contents

Acknowledgements   8
Editor's Note   9
Introduction   10
Glossary for non-journalists   18
Standfirst   21

Adjectives   47
Alliteration   51
And now   53
The asthmatic comma   57
Captions   64
Catchwords   68
Clichés (standard)   71
Clichés (trade)   73
Compression   76
Consequences   78
Crossheads   82
Dead letters   85
Dots and dashes   88
Dramatic events drama   93
Facetiousness   94
Free speech   103
Grammar   106
Great minds   111
How say you?   114
Hyphens   117
Illiterals   119
Imaginary rules   123
The incredible blob   127
Inelegant variation   128
The intro   131

Keith Waterhouse (1929-2009) was one of our most versatile and prolific writers. His long-running newspaper column, which appeared twice-weekly in the *Daily Mirror* and then in the *Daily Mail*, won many major press awards culminating in the *What the Papers Say* Lifetime Achievement Award in 2000. In 2004, he was voted Greatest Contemporary Columnist by the *British Journalism Review*. His hit play *Jeffrey Bernard is Unwell* won the *Evening Standard* Comedy of the Year Award for 1990. Other stage successes include *Mr and Mrs Nobody*, *Bookends* and *Our Song*. His widely acclaimed novels include *There is a Happy Land* (1957), *Billy Liar* (1959), *Jubb* (1963), *Maggie Muggins* (1981), *In the Mood* (1983), *Our Song* (1988), *Soho* (2001) and *Palace Pier* (2003). He recalled his early life and later career in two engaging memoirs: *City Lights* (1994) and *Streets Ahead* (1995). In collaboration with Willis Hall he wrote extensively for film, theatre and television, their credits including *Billy Liar*, *Whistle Down the Wind*, *A Kind of Loving*, and the long running TV series *Budgie* and *Worzel Gummidge*. Six collections of his journalism have been published.

Keith Waterhouse was made a CBE in 1991.

KEITH WATERHOUSE

WATERHOUSE ON NEWSPAPER STYLE

ILLUSTRATIONS BY TROG

Revel Barker
Publishing
www.booksaboutjournalism.com

First published by Viking, 1989
Published by Penguin Books, 1993

This revised edition, edited by Stella Bingham,
is published by
Revel Barker Publishing, 2010

ISBN: 978-0-9563686-9-0
Revel Barker Publishing
66 Florence Road
Brighton BN2 6DJ
England
revelbarker@gmail.com

I say, I say	135
Italic and bold	137
Jargon	140
Journalese	143
Just-so stories	146
Kneejerks	147
Lists	150
Little by little	155
Metaphor and simile	157
More haste	161
Not only but also	164
The numbers game	165
Officialese	168
Oh, really?	170
Ooh la la	172
Paragraphs	176
The pay-off	180
Person to person	182
Polysyllables	183
Puns and wordplay	186
Quote unquote	195
Ramboism	198
Rank and file	204
Says who?	209
Screamers!	211
Sexism	213
Sex romps	215
Stagger off	221
Supernumeraries	222
Tabloidese	223
Tautology	230
The tops	233
The weather-vane	236
What rot	238
Which is that?	241
What is style?	243

Acknowledgements

Grateful acknowledgement is made to the national and regional press for the examples of newspaper style quoted in this book.

Grateful acknowledgement is made to the estate of the late Mrs Sonia Brownell Orwell and Secker & Warburg Ltd for permission to quote from George Orwell's *Politics and the English Language*, first published in 1946.

Editor's Note

Waterhouse on Newspaper Style has been out of print for 13 years but demand for it, from universities and journalism schools, never ceased. Last year, when a reprint was proposed, Waterhouse was delighted and agreed to update it, 'removing titles of now-dead newspapers, defunct TV stars etc' but leaving the quotes and extracts as they stood. 'Most of them,' he wrote, 'belong to that timeless world of tabloidese and don't date at all'.

Sadly, Waterhouse died before he could carry out the work and the task fell to me. The publisher and I decided to leave it almost untouched, as a book of its time and a tribute to its author. Many chapters Waterhouse himself would have felt no need to update. Others, such as CAPTIONS, which focuses on the sadly diminished world of page three girls, now have a period charm.

Waterhouse on Newspaper Style is still the standard, and most entertaining, manual of tabloid journalism, as important and relevant today as when it was first published in 1989.

– Stella Bingham

Introduction

This handbook has had a somewhat unusual publishing history.

It started life as an in-house style book for journalists on the *Daily Mirror* and its sister papers, particularly new recruits – but with a difference. Most newspapers have a style book which lays down, for the sake of consistency, the paper's rules on spelling, punctuation, preferred use of upper or lower case initial letters and other usage, often peppered with random idiosyncrasies of editors and proprietors past and present. Thus do newcomers to *The Times*, for example, learn that the house spelling of *recognise* is *recognize*. Some style books are grander than others – for instance, the *Economist's Pocket Style Book* with its entertaining admonitions ('By all means begin an article hopefully, but never write *Hopefully, it will be finished by Monday*') runs to 100 pages, the Associated Press *Stylebook and Libel Manual* to 330. But while these useful volumes are on public sale, they remain essentially day-to-day reference books for the working journalists to whom they are addressed. *Daily Mirror Style – The Mirror's Way With Words*, as the manual came to be called, was intended from the start to be something more than a conventional newspaper style book. It was to be a polemic against tired, shoddy journalese and a plea for fresh, workmanlike writing – or as Roy Hattersley put it in a review in the *Listener* when the book finally 'went public', 'a missal as well as a manual, a testament as much as a textbook'.

Daily Mirror Style evolved from sporadic conversations over a period of months, indeed years, with two old friends – the then editor of the *Daily Mirror* (and later editor in chief of Mirror Group Newspapers), Michael Molloy, and the then chairman and editorial director of the group, Anthony Miles. I was at that time closely involved with the *Mirror*, writing a long-running, twice-weekly column (later transferred to the *Daily Mail*) as well as helping to produce occasional campaigning issues of the paper. I shared my colleagues' concern at the way the popular papers' use of language was developing, not to say deteriorating.

Finally, with the inducement that I could take myself off anywhere in the world to write it, Molloy persuaded me to marshal our collective thoughts, buttressed by specific examples of what we meant by bad workmanship, into a new kind of newspaper style book. And so off I went to San Francisco with, to the puzzlement of the United States Customs, a suitcase full of English tabloid newspapers. The manifesto was written quickly (Hattersley's review correctly attributes to deadline urgency what he calls 'the excitement' of *Daily Mirror Style*), and it was placed on the desk of every Mirror Group journalist a few weeks later, towards the end of 1979.

The book was produced in a plain white cover in an edition of 1,000 copies. It was gratifyingly well received in the *Mirror* office, even by old hands whose response understandably might have been that they didn't need lessons on how to suck eggs. Newcomers to the paper welcomed it as (so they told me) a rather more refreshing instruction manual than had hitherto come their way. Soon I heard that journalists on other newspapers were begging copies, albeit for amusement rather than enlightenment. *Daily Mirror Style*, as John Naughton was to note in the *Observer*, rapidly 'acquired something of a *samizdat* status in Fleet Street, with dog-eared copies changing hands for "considerations"'. The *New Statesman* rated its smuggled copy 'one of this office's most valued possessions'. The initial print run was soon exhausted, and *Mirror* recruits, for whom it was primarily intended, had to make do with tea-stained, cigarette-burned rejects left behind in the desk drawers of disillusioned old hacks who had taken redundancy and gone off to work as public relations consultants or to open village shops.

That was if they could find a copy. When I heard that they were now being run off (illegally, of course) on office photocopiers, I decided to explore the possibility of a publicly available edition. My then publishers were lukewarm: they felt that as it stood the manual was too specialized to command sales beyond Fleet Street. For my part, I had neither the time nor the inclination to adapt or modify it for the general reader. I was convinced that with its inky immediate flavour of the bustling newspaper office it had general reader appeal already – everyone likes a glimpse behind the scenes.

So it proved. Eventually the publishing wing of the Mirror Group, Mirror Books Ltd, hitherto specializing in cartoon collections and puzzle books, were persuaded (not without a little editorial arm-twisting, I fancy) to bring out a bookshop edition of 10,000 copies. Apart from the addition of a short introduction and glossary of some of the peculiar printers' and journalists' terms that had found their way into its pages, it was uncompromisingly and exactly as it had been originally published for circulation within the *Daily Mirror* office. The public edition even included, under the heading DOES ALL THIS MATTER?, what was essentially a private harangue to the more cynical members of the *Mirror*'s editorial staff:

> Yes.
>
> Every word that appears in the *Daily Mirror*, from the splash headline to the most obscure clue in the Quizword, has a byline – the byline of the *Daily Mirror*.
>
> The pitch of the *Mirror*'s voice reveals what it thinks of its readers. The voice-range runs from respect (the *Mirror* at its best) to apparent contempt (the *Mirror* at its worst).
>
> More important: the *Mirror*'s voice tells readers what they should think of the *Mirror*. Is it an interesting paper? An important paper? A silly paper? An essential paper? A paper worth buying every day? A paper worth cancelling?
>
> The constantly revised answers to such questions are to be found in the thirty or forty thousand words of the *Mirror*'s daily output. That is why this manual is considering that wordage in detail.

Mirror Books were not really geared to sending out review copies – I imagine that the Andy Capp and Perishers collections are little in demand among literary editors. I therefore turned myself into a cottage industry and personally despatched a few copies of the book to persons and papers I thought might be interested. Within a few weeks we had major reviews in *The Times Literary Supplement*, *The Times Educational Supplement*, the *Listener*, the *UK Press Gazette*, the *Journalist's Handbook*, the *Spectator*, the *Observer* and other journals – including even *World Medicine*, whose unpredicted recommendation was that 'it could benefit not only doctors who take refuge behind jargon, but also their frequently baffled patients'. The Cabinet Office bracketed it with Fowler's *Modern English Usage* and Partridge's *Usage and Abusage* as recommended reading in a pamphlet urging civil servants to use plain English.

Thanks to this quite extraordinary reception, plus its previously acquired almost underworld reputation in the taverns of Fleet Street, *Daily Mirror Style* quickly established itself as a standard textbook for journalism courses up and down the country, as well as a manual for teachers and students of English generally.

But when the Mirror Group came to change ownership, the Mirror Books subsidiary's brief dalliance with anything more cerebral than cartoons and puzzles was brought to an abrupt stop, and the last 3,000 copies of *Daily Mirror Style* still in stock were sold off to Simmonds, the Fleet Street booksellers whose specializations included textbooks on journalism. Under the Simmonds wing, the book continued to sell steadily until eventually this edition too was exhausted. A reprint seemed in order, but while my style book had won many friends it had lost a publisher. Once more, to the exasperation of the author, and thanks to the ubiquitous copying machine, *Daily Mirror Style* began to circulate in unauthorized *samizdat* editions. I did not know whether to be flattered or inflamed when on a train one day a student of journalism asked me to autograph a copy of *Daily Mirror Style* hot from the photocopier.

The orphaned manual remained officially out of print until, by one of those devious routes by which it was now well accustomed to travelling, and with a friendly push from my former literary editor Margaret Pringle, it came to the attention of Viking.

By now it was in some need of revision. News is ephemeral, as are most of the personalities who make the headlines, and so some of the examples quoted had become, nearly ten years on, so dated as to be well-nigh incomprehensible. (Some of them were incomprehensible to begin with. I was reluctant to 'axe', as we newspaper hands put it, such choice examples of tabloidese as JAIL THREAT TO DRUG ROW STONE, which could be read as a threat by a prison to drug a noisy Stone, presumably a Rolling one – but which proves to be a long-forgotten story about one of the Rolling Stones being given what the Canadian Justice Department believed to be a too lenient suspended sentence for a drug offence (*drug row*), for which they had rather (*jail threat*) he went to prison.)

Furthermore, I was no longer connected with the *Daily Mirror*, and so it would have been something of an impertinence to continue to hector my former colleagues, especially in front of a wider readership. This factor, and the knowledge that the manual was being widely used as a teaching aid on English courses, helped persuade me that in updating it I should address a greater audience directly rather than merely allowing them to eavesdrop, so to speak, on journalistic shoptalk.

Expanded, revised and updated, what started life as the *Mirror*'s in-house style book now blossoms forth, therefore, as a manual on newspaper style for the general reader with an interest in words as well as for journalists, trainee journalists, teachers and students of English. There are, and will be, copies for all. I trust that this edition will remain a stranger to the photocopying machine.

NOTE: One term I have not updated is 'Fleet Street' as a generic expression for the newspaper world. Although with the coming of new technology the national newspapers are now scattered far and wide, the term still seems as good as any.

Glossary for non-journalists

BILLBOARD. A display typeface of the kind once used on theatre and circus posters.

BLURB. An announcement, usually lavish in nature, of what is in store for the reader.

BODY-TYPE. The main typeface in which an article is set.

BOLD (or Boldface). Thick black type used for emphasis.

BROADSHEET. Large-format newspaper page the size of the *Daily Telegraph*.

BUSTING. A headline that is too long to fit the space available is said to 'bust'.

BYLINE. The printed acknowledgement – ranging from a simple line of type to 'star billing' complete with photograph – of the authorship of any piece of journalism.

CAPS. Capital letters.

CHARACTERS. Letters, figures, punctuation marks, etc.

CHIEF SUB. Executive who allocates and approves sub-editors' work.

CROSSHEADS. Occasional lines of type, usually bigger and bolder than the body-type, which are meant to liven up the page.

DEADLINE. The time by which a journalist must have his story filed if it is not to miss the next edition.

EM, EN. Units of measurement for type, being the width of the letters M or N.

FILE. To transmit copy to the paper.

FONT. A typeface of one particular style and size.

FOURTH ESTATE. Supposedly Fleet Street's place in the established order of things after the Lords Spiritual, the Lords Temporal and the Commons. ('The gallery in which the reporters sit has become a fourth estate of the realm' - Macaulay.)

GOTHIC. An elaborate typeface resembling medieval script.

HEAVIES. Popular journalists' faintly derisory term for supposedly serious papers such as *The Times* and the *Guardian*.

HOUSE STYLE. Standardized spelling, style of punctuation, policy on capital letters, etc., intended to be followed by everyone on the paper.

INTRO. Opening or introductory paragraph.

LEADED. Spaced out to fit the allocated length, in hot metal days literally by inserting blank slugs of lead between the lines of type.

LEG. A length of type as it appears on the page: a story occupying three columns would be said to be in three legs.

LITERAL. A typographical error. Sometimes called a typo.

LOWER CASE. Small letters, i.e. not capitals.

NIGHT LAWYER. Barrister who reads copy and proofs for possible libel.

PAGE SCHEME. A layout of a page showing the position of headlines, pictures, advertisements, etc.

PAR. Paragraph.

PAY-OFF. The last paragraph of a story, particularly if it contains a final twist or flourish.

POINT. (12-point, 144-point, etc.). Type measurement on the basis of 72 points to the inch.

QUOTE, QUOTES. Verbatim extract from a speech or interview. Quotation marks.

ROMAN. Plain upright letters (as opposed to italics).

SCREAMER. Exclamation mark.

SHY. Too short in length or width: a headline could be said to be two ems shy.

SPIKE. Depository for rejected copy.

SPLASH. Main front-page story.

STANDFIRST. Introductory matter that is separate from the story or feature itself.

STONE-SUB. The sub-editor who sees printed material in page form and cuts articles on the spot if they are too long to fit, as well as making last minute corrections. The stone was originally a stone slab – later a metal one – on which the page was assembled from type and photographic blocks.

SUB. Sub-editor who edits and checks articles and writes the headlines and crossheads.

SUB-DECK. A subsidiary headline.

UPPER CASE. Capital letters.

WIDOW. A line of type containing a single word or syllable.

Standfirst

Northcliffe's halfpenny *Daily Mail* was dismissed by the Prime Minister of the day, Lord Salisbury, as 'written by office boys for office boys'. Though the proficient newspaper technicians and university graduates among the new paper's staff might have resented the sneer, there was some truth in it. For a good forty years the popular press was to speak in a strange, celluloid-collar English peculiar to the clerical classes.

In those penny-a-lining days, policemen were upholders of the law, criminals were denizens of the underworld, goalkeepers were custodians of the citadel – and journalists were gentlemen of the press. They wrote like counting-house clerks forging their own references.

Long after the times had changed, the language of newspapers had not. This *Daily Mirror* headline tells us that the period is the Twenties: SHORT-LIVED ROMANCE OF WELL-TO-DO WIDOW AND A COCKTAIL SHAKER. But the accompanying report could have been written in the eighteen-nineties: 'In the Divorce Court yesterday, Mr Justice Hill granted a decree nisi to Mrs Ellen O'Connor, residing at Lancaster Gate, W., in consequence of the misconduct of her husband... '

Meanwhile, what are now sometimes called the text newspapers – *The Times,* the *Daily Telegraph,* the *Morning Post,* etc. – continued to address their readership in what they would have claimed was the voice of the educated man, but which it would be nearer the mark to say was the voice of the educated policeman giving evidence. To the modern ear, the tone no longer seems all that different from that of the Northcliffe *Daily Mail* and its imitators. Nor, substantially, was it, for the voice of the popular press was essentially an obsequious imitation of its elders and betters.

Two influences were to drag newspaper style slamming and blasting into the twentieth century – the *Daily Mirror* and the *Daily Express.*

The *Mirror* was the first British newspaper to revolt against the strangulated police court prose in which journalists felt impelled to write. The story of how it did so has been well told in Hugh Cudlipp's *Publish and be Damned* and need not be re-summarized here. It is enough to say that in the mid Thirties the *Mirror* spat the plum from its mouth and began to speak in its own down-to-earth voice. (Although the voice was still not averse to the odd imitation, as a blurb for the popular Beezlebub Jones strip cartoon shows: 'Zeke was plumb kayoed by the bonk on the cabeezer which Davy done give him with his wooden laig...' Several decades after Beezlebub's demise, expressions of the *plumb loco* variety are to be found only in old dictionaries of American slang – and in the columns of current British popular newspapers.)

The *Daily Mirror*, to borrow some favourite expressions from its new robust vocabulary, ceased to be fuddy-duddy and became brash and cheeky. Or so it seemed at the time: from a distance of more than half a century, its snappy captions have the wistful charm of old sepia photographs:

WELL, OF ALL THE LUCK

On the hottest day of the year, these two girls set out for a day's work in the film studio at Denham.

And found that their job was to be photographed in their undies for the film 'Ten Days in Paris'.

And if that isn't luck on a blazing day, we'd like to know what luck is.

Sometimes, it has to be said with hindsight, the paper's efforts to be bright and breezy had all the desperation of a fixed smile, and on occasion, anticipating the antics of today's tabloids, it could be so trivial as to appear featherbrained. The self-conscious, over-staccato language, striving to be up-to-date and down-to-earth at the same time, oscillated wildly between the slangy and the streamlined, the homely and the Hollywood. But at its best it was good, plain, refreshing, vigorous English. It was not, as has sometimes been claimed, 'the language of the people', for just as the people had never called criminals denizens of the underworld nor goalkeepers custodians of the citadel, neither did they now call psychiatrists mind-doctors nor professors egg-heads, nor drop the definite article from the beginnings of sentences ('Box with documents buried sixty-four years ago has been unearthed during repairs at...'). But it was language the people could understand.

Beaverbrook's *Daily Express*, the other innovator, was at about the same time pioneering the bright and breezy approach to broadsheet journalism. Its legendary editor Arthur Christiansen, very much his master's voice but none the less past master of the voice in which his master's paper spoke, perfected package journalism – the story brought in by the reporter being merely the raw product to be processed, prettified, wrapped in cellophane and tied up in ribbon by the sub-editor assigned to it. Some *Express* writer-subs became

personalities, famous in Fleet Street i
outside it for their manipulation of raw ᵔᵔ
material to fit a particular spot in the paper. The
Daily Express was not about news, but about its
presentation – which was brilliant. The
summation of the Christiansen technique was
perhaps when Sir Edmund Hillary, as he was
about to become, ascended Mount Everest
triumphantly – but very inconveniently for Fleet
Street which had cleared its front pages for the
Coronation of Her Majesty Queen Elizabeth II.
The headline that got the *Express* off the horns of
a news priority dilemma was journalistic genius:
⌈ALL THIS – AND EVEREST TOO!⌋

The new language of the mass circulation
press had an effect on journalism that went far
beyond calling a spade a spade instead of a
gardening implement. Between the maverick,
anti-establishment, Empire-preference Toryism
of Beaverbrook and the barrack-room
bolshieism of the *Daily Mirror*, a revolution of
sorts was going on. When reporters stopped
calling policemen upholders of the law and
started calling them cops (in the movie slang of
the day, or the tabloid slang of today), it was not
only Fleet Street's musty terminology they were
beginning to question. If it was not the end of
political favouritism – that day is yet to come – it

was the end of automatic forelock-tugging deference to the great and the good.

The Uriah Heep approach typified by the *Mirror*'s coverage of the 1929 election – 'A further succession of Socialist gains was the unhappy tale of yesterday's election results' – had now gone for ever. Authority was no longer kowtowed to. Institutions were challenged. Emperors wearing new clothes were told unkind home truths. Applecarts were upset. Cassandra, the *Mirror*'s great columnist, was billed as 'the terror of the twerps'. Sledgehammer text accompanied piledriver headlines. And when the *Mirror* and *Express* were not engaged in their respective favourite pastimes of taunting the 'fuddy-duddies' and persecuting a shortlist of Beaverbrook *bêtes noires* headed by Lord Mountbatten, both papers indulged in their other celebrated preoccupation of remorselessly having Fun. (The *Daily Mirror*, in particular, periodically pursued Fun with the dedication of an alcoholic on a three-day jag.)

Fleet Street would never be the same again. But the *Mirror* and *Express* between them had not only tossed a hand grenade into that hitherto cloistered thoroughfare; they had lit a fuse for a greater revolution yet. For as Tom Baistow notes in his critical anatomy of Fleet Street, *Fourth Rate Estate*, 'The basic principle of

Christiansen's formula journalism, shaping news and features to a predetermined "exciting" image, prepared Fleet Street for the next generic change, the mass conversion to tabloid format.'

Tabloid, a term registered in 1884 by what is now the Wellcome Foundation Ltd as a trademark applied to chemical substances, and held by the Court of Appeal to be a 'fancy word', appears to this day [1989] in the *UK Press Gazette*'s list of registered trademarks requiring a capital initial. But in its secondary, lower-case definition in the *Shorter Oxford English Dictionary* – 'a newspaper of small format which gives its news in concentrated form 1926' – it has long been identified with what politicians like to call 'certain sections of the press'.

All the mass circulation papers are by now tabloid in size except for the *Sunday Express*, which toyed with the idea of abandoning its broadsheet format but decided against it. But what *is* a tabloid newspaper? The Audit Bureau of Circulation (ABC) lumps the total daily sales of the popular papers at around 12 million [1989 figures], as against about 2½ million for the *Daily Telegraph*, the *Guardian*, *The Times*, the *Independent* and the *Financial Times*; and about 15 million total Sunday sales for the populars compared with nearly 3 million for the *Sunday Times*, the *Observer* and the *Sunday Telegraph*. But when we consider that the list of tabloid daily titles includes the *Daily Mail*, the *Daily Express*, and *Today* [1986-1995] along with the *Sun*, the *Daily Star*, and the *Daily Mirror*, and that the Sunday titles include the *Mail on Sunday* as well as the *News of the World*, the *Sunday Mirror* and the *People*, not to mention their strange bedfellow the *Sunday Sport* ('World War 2's best-kept secret – ADOLF HITLER WAS A WOMAN'), then the classification becomes meaningless except in its original definition – 'a newspaper of small format'. What we really mean by the tabloids, or what we primarily mean, and certainly what our guardians of morality and decent standards mean when castigating the 'gutter press', are the *Sun*, the *Daily Star*, the *Daily Mirror*, the *News of the World*, the *Sunday Mirror* and the *People* – in other words what might be termed the red-top tabloids.

But even within this definition there are shades of meaning. The *Daily Mirror*, as its editor has been at pains to point out in a testy letter to the *Independent*, considers itself in a class apart from the *Sun* and the *Daily Star*. The *Sunday Mirror* might likewise claim, although with less conviction, that any similarity between itself and the *News of the World* and the *People*, is purely coincidental. As for the other papers, the

Daily Express and *Today* might be described as near-to-distant cousins of the red-tops (both papers' authentic tabloid-style content varies from day to day), while the *Daily Mail'*s place on the family tree would be between the *Daily Telegraph* and the *Express*, and the *Mail on Sunday* next to its rival the *Sunday Express*. But when the *Sunday Times* book review section can headline a serious analysis of the Booker Prize shortlist FOR LOVE OF LITERATURE AND LOADSAMONEY (see CATCHWORDS) and the *Daily Telegraph* can report, in a story headed FRENCH LEARN TO POT THEIR REDS, that there was a Gallic row the day Le Snooker came to France (see FACETIOUSNESS), then it is apparent that tabloid style has by now infiltrated – some would say infested – all newspapers, tabloid or broadsheet, popular or 'quality', to a greater or lesser extent. Even the *Financial Times* cannot resist reporting that a plan to impose charges for horse grazing to raise money for a local health authority is a drop in the hay bucket, or headlining the story HOSPITAL USES HORSE SENSE TO RAISE CASH (see PUNS AND WORDPLAY). Only the *Independent*, the newest of the national newspapers, can claim immunity.

Even more significantly, tabloid journalism has had the most profound effect on regional newspapers, particularly the evenings. While (or so one hopes) there will always be some corners of the provincial press where councillors take up cudgels, irate residents are up in arms, veterans are ninety years young, youths involved in a fracas sustain injuries, drivers of vehicles which were in collision are very poorly, and court cases are headlined MAN, 36, ON GRAVE CHARGE, many of the regional papers have become but teething rings for cub journalists with ambitions to work on one of the tabloids when they grow up. The rot set in when the women's pages first saw the headings HELLO TO GOOD BUYS and KNITTING PRETTY. Now, with a remorseless facetiousness worthy of the *Sun* itself, the *Western Mail* report of a spaghetti-eating contest began: 'Mama Mia! Champion spaghetti-eater Salvatore Intrigiza gulped down four pounds of the stuff in just three minutes yesterday... ' The *Shropshire Star* came close to its Fleet Street namesake in reporting that 'Shropshire mayors thought it a blooming good idea when the county's Horticultural Society presented them with £50,000 worth of floral planters to brighten up their towns.' The same paper's headline on a story about the vicar's decision to silence the church clock's quarterly chimes was TOWN'S STRIKING FEATURE STRUCK OFF. Not to be outdone, the *Bristol Evening Post*'s headline on a report on an owl protection scheme was WISE

MOVES OVER BARN OWLS. The *Burnley Express* had a rare example of the tabloid technique being put to clever use: HIGH NOON FOR THE TAXI COWBOYS.

Even the once staid, fatstock-price-riddled rural weeklies are not immune. Side by side with the well-worn, reassuring DOG BIT PAPERBOY, the *Bucks Herald* had PEDDLING THE CASE FOR MORE CYCLE WAYS; and, in a rather endearing if baffling attempt to inject tabloid facetiousness into the text, 'All's well on the western front, or rather on the roads leading to Stoke Mandeville railway station.'

Gresham's Law applies to the press as much as to any other commercial force – perhaps, in view of its communicative nature, more so. The pure, not to say puritan, prose of the text papers has been diluted, not to say defiled, by the example of the tabloids. The tabloids themselves have gone downmarket of one another, the *Sun* and the *Daily Star* vying to out-parody themselves, and the *Daily Mirror*, on occasion, aping the *Sun* like a rebellious convent girl who has seen a Bette Davis film slashing her face with lipstick. Even Britain's bawdy answer to the American *National Inquirer*, the *Sunday Sport*, which runs advertisements no real newspaper would touch ('Dirty dialling for you. Just put your finger in the hole') and 'stories' no real newspaper would print (B25 BOMBER FOUND ON MOON), can be said to be exerting an influence on the *News of the World*, which is now happy, or anyway willing, to publish such stomach-churning material as HORROR OF THE PICKLED BABIES – WEIRD COUPLE KEEP DEAD TOTS IN JAR TO CHAT WITH.

It is apparent, then, that any examination of newspaper style has to start with tabloid journalism, its most pervasive influence.

This is not to be considered, however, a crusade against tabloid journalism, Tabloid style can be a benevolent as well as a malignant growth on the language structure of newspapers. As perfected by the *Daily Mirror* and developed by the *Daily Express*, tabloid prose at its best – excitable, exuberant, always vigorous, sometimes vitriolic – is a lively and valuable asset to the language. At its worst – as when the *Sun* heavy-handedly and meaninglessly reports about a couple who tried to get a refund for the Balkan holiday where they were served stewed pork twice a day, 'But the holiday organizers have given them the chop' – it is plain silly.

Nor are the tabloids themselves to be held up to ridicule or contempt simply for being tabloids. Their contribution to journalism is

considerable. Lord Rees-Mogg, a former edit
of *The Times*, comparing the *Sun* for its
'remarkable professional achievement' with the
Daily Mirror and the *Daily Express* in their
heyday, has described its editor Kelvin
MacKenzie as 'as good a technician as Arthur
Christiansen'. With professional detachment,
one can judge their technical achievements
without necessarily endorsing their philosophy.
One does not have to support the *Sun*'s gung-ho
position, for instance, to appreciate,
journalistically speaking, that GOTCHA!, while
tasteless and guilty of RAMBOISM, was the most
memorable headline of the Falklands campaign.

The tabloids are vulgar, of course. But then if
they were not vulgar they would not be
tabloids. The creed of the *Daily Mirror*, printed
as a front-page manifesto by its editor from 1948
to 1953, Silvester Bolam, could be the creed for
all tabloids – if they cared to live up to it:

> The *Mirror* is a sensational newspaper. We
> make no apology for that. We believe in the
> sensational presentation of news and views,
> especially important news and views, as a
> necessary and valuable public service in these
> days of mass readership and democratic
> responsibility.
>
> We shall go on being sensational to the best of
> our ability...

Sensationalism does not mean distorting the truth. It means vivid and dramatic presentation of events so as to give them a forceful impact on the mind of the reader. It means big headlines, vigorous writing, simplification into familiar everyday language, and the wide use of illustration by cartoon and photograph...

Every great problem facing us – the world economic crisis, diminishing food supplies, the population puzzle, the Iron Curtain and a host of others – will only be understood by the ordinary man busy with his daily tasks if he is hit hard and often with the facts...

As in larger, so in smaller and more personal affairs, the *Mirror* and its millions of readers prefer the vivid to the dull and the vigorous to the timid.

No doubt we make mistakes, but we are at least alive.

No one would claim that the tabloids of today do not make mistakes – particularly mistakes of taste and judgement. But this manual's concern is with the standards of English in journalism, not with the standards of journalism itself. The two are, of course, intertwined. Either can drag the other up – or down. When the *Sun* reports OH! @X! BABY'S FIRST WORD IS BUGGER or boasts that all the breast news is in the *Sun*, it is consciously readjusting, in a downward direction, what is deemed acceptable in the newspapers of today. But as to standards, ethics, accuracy, invasion of privacy and so on, it is for others to call upon the tabloids to 'put their house in order', to use the favourite phrase of their detractors.

Neither is newspaper content any of this manual's business. Again, content and the language in which that content is written cannot be entirely divorced from one another. Many of the worst excesses of tabloid journalism arise out of its peculiar news values, where material is often selected simply because it is seen as suitable for the full tabloid treatment. The kind of 'news' stories discussed under FACETIOUSNESS are 80, sometimes 99 per cent froth. Once the decision has been made to publish the type of stuff discussed under SEX ROMPS, a style has to be evolved to get the maximum out of the story without being arrested for it. But our main concern here must be not with what newspapers write but how they write it.

What, then, is this peculiar form of English we are calling tabloid style (not entirely to be confused with TABLOIDESE)? It is a patois made up of unconsidered trifles. It could be compared, irreverently, with those ransom notes which are made up of lettering cut from various publications. Tabloid style takes its references from a wide variety of sources – TV shows, film titles, advertising slogans, sporting events, song lyrics, political jargon, catchphrases, clichés (including, cannibalistically, many of its own invention), and that vast repository at large of popular quotations, rhymes and snatches, which it juggles into a deft montage of puns, allusions and wordplay. (Although the tabloids are reckoned to need a reading age of around ten, understanding them requires a high degree of sophistication and recognition of often subtle or obscure allusions; when the *News of the World* sets up a headline MUCKY JIM, it does so in the confidence that most of its readers will be familiar with the title of a novel taken by Kingsley Amis from a music-hall song.)

We have already seen that in inexperienced hands the end product can be truly awful. In experienced hands it can be even worse. The archetypal tabloid story is a piece of high-precision engineering, with the predictability accurate to a thousandth of an inch, the hackneyed phraseology polished like old brass, and old puns worn smooth with age gliding effortlessly into place like moving parts of a well-oiled Victorian donkey engine.

While the style is one of the most difficult of English idioms to master (not that many outside the newspaper world have any desire to do so – but those who do attempt it, particularly populist academics, usually make a hash of it), it is highly addictive. Not only does it quickly enslave innocent provincial tyros who want to make their mark, it so clouds the judgement of its hardened practitioners that they are reduced to giggling self-parody (hence headlines of the FREDDIE STARR ATE MY HAMSTER variety, the red-top equivalent of the NUDE VICAR HAD CORNFLAKES BOX ON HEAD type of headlines with which bored subs used to amuse themselves in the *News of the World*'s old broadsheet days). Eventually, the style so has them in its grip that, by now incapable of any creative thought above the banal, they find themselves victims of a kind of premature journalistic senility, degenerating rapidly via promotional bingo slogans like IF YOU WIN OUR LOTTO POTTO YOU CAN FLY TO SOMEWHERE HOTTO to infantile rhyming news headlines such as WACKO JACKO TURNS HIS BACKO ON ANGRY KIMMO, MICKIE IN NICKIE, BURT IN £1M GRINGO STINGO and EASY ON THE BURGIE, FERGIE. The tabloids have often been criticized – or 'lambasted', as they would say – for their so-called 'bonk journalism'. Their *Beano* journalism has almost as much to answer for.

In *Beano* journalism the tabloids are to be seen herding themselves into a cul-de-sac where their mutant form of tabloidism could surely, given time, only wither and die. But is the picture any healthier out on the main thoroughfare?

Popular journalism – as H. L. Mencken acknowledges in his scholarly *The American Language,* even though his stuffier counterparts on this side of the Atlantic may not – used to be one of the great invigorating influences on the language (there is a plaque in Times Square to the sports cartoonist who coined 'hot dog'). Today it is one of the most deadening influences. Happily, this negative influence is in the main only upon journalism itself. It is remarkable, and significant, that a style so assiduously and incestuously imitated within the newspaper world should have made so little impact outside it. As noted elsewhere in these pages, the language to which half the population is exposed daily is spoken by nobody. Its theoretically punchy vocabulary is simply not part of the common tongue. Only on the TV and radio news bulletins does one hear tabloidese actually giving voice ('Good evening. The dollar takes a pounding') – and there, news and current affairs executives are vigorous in their determination to wean their reporters and news-readers from clapped-out tabloid clichés back to good spoken English. The BBC *Style Guide* on news scripts for regional TV and local radio wittily pinpoints some of the tabloidisms that have crept into bulletins: '*Gutted*: burnt out (unless your script is about fish). *Inferno*: fire. Consign *inferno* to it along with *blaze*. *Mercy dash*: no, no. *Set*: in a recent script Prince Charles was 'set to step into a row'. *Set* in this context is journalese. Try to confine its use to jellies and tea-tables… '

With some notable exceptions – not all of them the star writers who have *carte blanche* to use expressions like *carte blanche* – the contribution of popular journalism to the language over fifty years has consisted only of, in the immortal words of Ernest Bevin, 'clitch after clitch after clitch' – which have not even been accepted into common parlance. In an age when ordinary street English grows ever more expressive and colourful, journalism is suffering from stunted growth.

It is tempting to quote fancy theories as to what has gone wrong. One is that in our more sophisticated times we no longer live in a black-and-white world tailor-made for crusading tabloids, and that as the issues of the day grow ever more complex (and incidentally more likely to be covered at length by the TV documentary), the tabloids retreat into trivia, with a resultant trivialisation of their once trenchant style. Another is that competition has raised the tabloid voice to such a monotonously shrill level that it has lost its impact (note that raising the voice is not the same as raising the tone).

There is probably something in both these notions. Certainly competition between the red tops often seems confined to who can shout the loudest about the same 'exclusive'. On the trivia level, the steady retreat of the tabloids, and to an extent their provincial imitators, into the semi-fantasy land of showbiz, where the distinction between the on-screen and off-screen exploits of soap stars is so blurred that when readers see the strapline EASTENDERS EXCLUSIVE – THE *REAL* INSIDE STORY OF SOAP STAR'S LIFE BEHIND BARS they wonder momentarily whether this is a real-life story or a real television script, has had a consequential blunting effect on the precision of the reportage brought to the task.

The apparently bottomless market for stories about the ever-expanding royal family has similarly been exploited to the detriment of true tabloid style. When a royal baby was born, the *Independent* judged that the news warranted a three-line item on an inside page – or anyway, decided to make it a three-line item on an inside page, which is not necessarily the same thing. The *Sun* – styled *Royal Baby Sun* on that day's masthead – gave the event seven pages, the *Daily Star* gave it four, and the *Daily Mirror* six –

plus the promise of a colour souvenir Royal Baby issue the next day. Even allowing for the indispensability of the child's family tree, her astrological chart, the tie-in with bingo ('Even Fergie's baby can play it!') and the *Sun*'s valiant attempt, headed A NAPPY LANDING, to outdo McGonegal ('Into a sunny world she bounces, Ouch! She weighs 6 pounds 12 ounces'), there are simply not that number of column inches to be got out of even a royal birth of the first importance (and this was not) without considerable padding. Thus the tabloids, to meet what rightly or wrongly they figured was the popular demand for such an excess of space, were bound to resort to tabloidism at its frothiest and silliest. The *Sun* again, on one of its main news pages: 'SHE'S TOP OF THE POPPETS. Hi there, tot pickers! It's the new Royal Chart Show and what a chart we've got for you. We've got three non-movers in the accession list, six losers and a sensational new entry – in at No. 5. It's the new release from Prince (Andrew, that is) – New York, New York, rocketing right into the top ten... ' And so on, to the extent of twelve column inches.

But there is another, more mundane, explanation for the decline of the tabloid style. Tabloid journalism, whatever giant steps it may imagine itself to be taking, is no longer doing anything new. The pioneer days are long over. When journalists arrive on a tabloid paper they no longer have to rethink their reporting or subbing style to its very basics, with that resultant jolt to the creative system that has produced some of Fleet Street's finest writers and editorial technicians over the years. They already know tabloid style, or what they have been told is tabloid style, backwards. They learned it on their very first suburban weeklies. There is not a junior reporter in the land who cannot churn out, 'Feathers really flew the night a chicken-sexer got the bird', or 'High Street shoppers went potty when they heard planners had gone round the bend and flushed them out of their public loo'. Recruits to Fleet Street are entitled to ask what need there is to learn new tricks when the old ones are still so much in demand.

How long the situation will remain so is anybody's guess. Lord Rees-Mogg, in the same article in the *Independent* in which he praised the *Sun* as a remarkable professional achievement, went on to say:

> There have been four dominant mass newspapers in this century. Each has aged with its proprietor – Northcliffe, Beaverbrook, [Cecil] King and now Murdoch. Each has depended heavily on its proprietor's personal force. Each

has lost its lead as Britain's social mix changed. So may the *Sun*, which faces both television competition and the coming to national majority of the new mass middle class which does not talk in the *Sun*'s strident demotic tone.

The leading popular paper of the twenty-first century will have its dark side – perhaps more like Beaverbrook's than Murdoch's – but I would expect it to turn the *Sun*'s flank by a more modern approach to a more modern audience. It will resemble Saatchi and Saatchi where the *Sun* is like an earthy Victorian music-hall. In Britain, the middle class always wins in the end.

We shall see. It takes some effort of the imagination to visualize the end of the six-pack lager culture which in turn would bring about a decline in the fortunes of the *Sun* and the *Daily Star*. But then in the *Daily Mirror*'s heyday it was difficult to see the traditional cloth-cap working class from which the *Mirror* drew its strength ever withering away. (But when the *Mirror* editorial management did see that times were changing, they turned the old TUC carthorse *Daily Herald* into a middlebrow paper called the *Sun*, aimed at an emerging educated class – the 'polyocracy' – which failed, however, to buy it. The *Sun* went for a knockdown price to Rupert Murdoch who suffered few illusions about the effects of education on a mass market.)

But the question is, anyway, what kind of middle class will it be that does the winning in the end? Middle-class tastes, never very high, are lowering all the time under the influence of the mass media and consumer advertising, and with the decline in educational standards. Good prose is not a first requirement. By a Saatchi and Saatchi approach Rees-Mogg presumably means a paper geared to reader interests such as holidays and leisure pursuits which would attract advertising revenue. But will such a paper be better written? With the notable exception of the *Independent*, new papers tend to be worse written. *Today* is well produced but sloppily written; there is no evidence that readers care about or even notice what would once have been regarded as a major flaw. The fact is that newspapers do not generally aim to attract new readers with good, crisp, straightforward writing. They aim to put on sales with colour, fatter magazines, more supplements, and expensive serializations.

While it is conceivable that with the by no means inevitable decline of the red tops will come a decline in the worst excesses of tabloidism, not only is tabloidese and tabloid influence bound to linger on (and indeed, within reasonable bounds, it is desirable that it should) but there is no reason to suppose that the standards of newspaper English will automatically rise.

What, then, is to be done? The *Daily Mirror* transformed the language of journalism in or around November 1934. It was as different from the language once used by newspapers as that of commercial radio is from the BBC English of the Reith era. But what is done first can only be done once. Revolutions do not go on happening. There can be but one revolution, and everything that follows (as the editor of the Peking *People's Daily* would doubtless agree) is merely revision.

No latterday Hugh Cudlipp, and certainly no Rupert Murdoch, is likely to shake up the popular press as thoroughly as it was shaken up over seventy years ago. It is easier to throw in a new colour magazine. Someone may invent a totally new kind of paper, but invention is something more than transformation. While the mass-circulation, nationally distributed dailies and Sundays last, it will be, give or take a supplement or two, in something pretty well approximate to their present form.

What the modern newspaper can do is to get better. It can take stock of itself. It can spring-clean. It can throw out much of its cliché-ridden, pun-barnacled vocabulary and invest in a good modern supply of plain English. It can dismantle ancient, cor-blimey hot metal headlines which have become as familiar as the neon signs in Piccadilly Circus. It can re-examine the stereotyped news values that encourage stereotyped writing – and the stereotyped writing that encourages stereotyped observation. It can, in sum, stop selling itself, and its readers short.

The object of this manual is to start hacking away at the dead wood.

Adjectives

Adjectives should not be allowed in newspapers unless they have something to say.

Red-haired tells us that a person has red hair. *Vivacious* – a word belonging to the lost world of Marcel waves and cocktail cherries – tells us nothing except that someone has sat down at a computer and keyed in the word 'vivacious'.

An adjective should not raise questions in the reader's mind, it should answer them. *Angry* informs. *Tall* invites the question, how tall? The well-worn phrase *His expensive tastes ran to fast cars* simply whets the appetite for examples of the expensive tastes, and the makes and engine capacity of the fast cars.

Adjectives used for effect should not be too clapped-out to evoke anything in the reader's mind: *grim* timetable of death, *vital* clues, *brutal* murder, *hush-hush* inquiry, no longer add very much to the nouns they accompany.

Smothering an intro in a ketchup of adjectives does little to improve its flavour – as when we read that Manchester City are poised to sign Wolves' *brilliant* midfield man and Wrexham's *impressive* striker in a *massive* £1m *double* deal. [1989 figures] *Massive*, like *double*, is TAUTOLOGY, compounded when we learn in the next paragraph that *the Maine Road club* (see INELEGANT VARIATION) are determined to push through the *massive* deal involving £880,000 for one player and £350,000 for the other. Then we are told that other clubs have been keen on the *impressive* lower-priced player. The repetition of an already inessential adjective is lame.

For a profession that is supposed to be hard-boiled, journalism is remarkably chivalrous with its adjectives. Models are *attractive* or *stunning*, or they are given the accolade of *top* (see THE TOPS), or they are *curvy*, a description that seems to have come into vogue when it dawned on someone that *curvaceous* was getting long in the tooth (so is *curvy* by now). Small young women are *petite*. Small old women are tiny. Young men are often *dashing*, an anyone-for-tennis word from the same era as *vivacious* – though macho men are these days more likely to be *hunky*. There are few ordinary housewives, but *model* housewives abound. The *Daily Mirror* has even given

us a *model* soldier: 'Model soldier John Jones i
made homeless – by the Army.' Long exposu
Mirror's weakness for model housewives arouses the
suspicion that this is not a story from Toytown.

Model may be a noun, adjective or verb. A further
suspicion about the above example is that it is a
noun masquerading as an adjective. A glance at any
day's papers (*MIRACLE* WIFE WHO 'DIED',
DANGER FOOD FIRMS RAPPED, *DREAM* TRIP TO
PARADISE) will show that nouns are used as
adjectives far more than adjectives proper. There is
nothing wrong with that: a considerable acreage of
pulp forest must have been saved over the years by
the use of *flight chaos* as shorthand for *chaos caused by
a strike of air traffic controllers* (but see TABLOIDESE and
RANK AND FILE). But the principle laid down at the
beginning of this section still applies. Bearing in
mind that an adjective by any name still has a proper
job to do, a noun used as an adjective should ideally
make a statement rather than raise a question.

Dawn swoop, though a choice example of
tabloidese, has something to say: it tells us roughly
at what time of day the swoop was made. *Surprise
swoop* raises the question, who was surprised? (It is
also tautology, since swoops are not normally made
by appointment.) *Shock swoop* is as bad as *surprise
swoop*, with the bonus fault that *shock* is a much
overused noun-adjective (*shock* report, *shock* move,
etc.).

Another over-used noun-adjective is *luxury*. Is it
worth mentioning that a Saudi Arabian prince lives

in a *luxury* home? We would hardly expect him to live in a barrel (which would be worth a line or two). But his *25-bathroom home* or his *£5m home* would be informative. *Luxury*, incidentally, has been for so long used as an adjective that some journalists have forgotten the proper meanings of its legitimately adjectival offshoots. The *Daily Mirror* invited competition winners to relax *luxuriantly* for a week on palm-fringed sands. *Luxuriant* means abundant or exuberant in growth. A *luxurious* week would have been a better offer.

Miracle is also over-used. In its day the *Mirror* has vouchsafed so many miracle wives, miracle mums, miracle babies, miracle cures and miracle escapes that an apposite consolation prize for competition runners-up not qualifying for a luxuriant week on palm-fringed sands could well be a year's supply of loaves and fishes.

Alliteration

Apt alliteration's artful aid has come to the rescue of many a hard-pressed sub-editor – nowhere more so than on page three, where Adorable Angie, Busty Babs, Curvy Caren, Dashing Debra, Gorgeous Gayner, Jaunty Jane, Luscious Lucy, Marvellous Melanie, Pouting Paula, Shapely Sharon, Terrific Tracey *et al.* hold court (see CAPTIONS); and in the sports pages (or Sizzling Super Sport Specials) where the likes of Blue Baird, Classy Carson, Glorious Gower, Kidding Kelly, Lionheart Lawrence, Mad Mike, Naff Nigel, Super Seaman, Tasty Taylor and Wonder Woosie are called to account, aided and abetted by such headlines as BRAZIL BOUT, SNAKE SOUP, GOLDEN GLOVES, FAB: FERGIE WAS

RIGHT TO RISK ROO, CRAZY CASH FOR COTTEE, SENNA'S SICKENER, WOOSIE'S A WOW, SMITH SPEND SPREE and TROUBLED TYSON IN £25M TUSSLE.

Elsewhere in a typical week's papers we may learn How Holly Hooked her Hunk; of the Sweeney Sarge Who Went Astray to become a Crooked Copper; of Sexy Sam's Svengali; of the Cost of Kitting out Kids for Class; how Blind Date Janet was Spurned by Super Star; how Troubled TV-AM is a real Turn-off; and of a Love-tug Legacy of Hate and Hope. It is not unusual for bungling burglars, confused cops, pampered pooches, randy rockers and tragic tots to make their appearance in the same paper on the same day. On the *News of the World*, the letter B seems to have an alliterative attraction, as in I BEDDED BUSTY BABS, THE BILL'S BRUTE BEAT ME BLACK AND BLUE, and BINGE KILLS BOOZY BOSS.

Like many another literary device, alliteration is best used sparingly, serendipity being a better inspiration – as in the Daily Mirror's LEGGY LOVELY LANDS UP LEGLESS – than midnight oil. It is to be doubted whether *Cigarette-sucking Henry Cecil was sending up smoke signals before a steward's inquiry cleared his flying filly* came to a *Star* sports sub in a frenzied flash.

And now

We were taught at school that we may not begin sentences with 'And'.

Then we were taught in newspaper offices that we may.

And quite right too. But newspapers so overdo it that they sometimes read like the New English Bible:

> As temperatures in the city soared to 81 F, it just wasn't a day to quibble about the Budget's 2p extra on a pint.
>
> *And* the hottest favourite at Royal Ascot was a chilled bottle of bubbly – at £19.50 a time. [1989 price]
>
> The top-hat-and-tails brigade sweltered in the sun.
>
> But the Queen clearly didn't reckon it was a day for dressing up.
>
> She stayed cool in the same outfit she wore on her trip to Saudi Arabia in February.
>
> *And* she cut 2ft off the hemline to give it a new look.
>
> The only people not revelling in the sun yesterday were hay-fever sufferers.
>
> The pollen count in the South East soared from a sniffling 33 – to an eye-watering 145.
>
> *And* the heat has also taken its toll on the Continent.
>
> The Greeks are being grilled by temperatures of 100F.
>
> At least thirteen people have died of sunstroke.

And it's like a Turkish bath in Istanbul ...

Besides being a near-perfect example of the chirpy weather round-up (see THE WEATHER VANE) this extract very well illustrates a common application of *and* – which is to round the edges of a piece that would otherwise have had too many sharp corners, caused by a succession of monotonously unvarying short sentences. The four *ands* could be removed from their present positions and placed in front of four other sentences, more or less at random, without affecting the story in any degree.

And is also commonly used to round off a sequence of events where the story takes a narrative form ('*And* last night the 35-year-old company director fell into bed – for a three-day rest'). Or it is used to split an over-long intro into two paragraphs ('*And* last night police were hunting three youths').

A close runner-up to *and* is *now*. Now what *now* is often really saying is 'Now read on':

> The sweet smell of success has turned into a right stinker of a problem for Kathy and Paul Johnson.
>
> The couple do a roaring trade in the smelliest stink bombs in town at their joke shop in New Street, Worcester.
>
> But the husband and wife team have upset other shopkeepers – because some of their customers have been letting the bombs off in other stores around the town.
>
> *Now* some irate shopkeepers have been carrying out revenge raids on the joke shop. The jokers will pose as ordinary customers, buy their

stink bombs... and burst the bombs on the shop floor...

In the first three paragraphs, we learn little more than that a joke shop sells stink bombs. *Now* brings us to the point of the story – in paragraph four.

The delayed-drop *now* is very common, and is often a case of the rules of CONSEQUENCES being bent to accommodate a story that wants to pass itself off as a narrative story but isn't one really.

Sometimes the two biblical devices are used in conjunction:

> Screen tough guy Charles Bronson is making his life a misery...
>
> *And now* he's doing something about it... He and fellow hard-man George C. Scott have formed a vigilante 'swat squad' to fight the menace...
>
> The problem is caused by a nearby sewage treatment plant which they say attracts the insects.
>
> *And* they claim that the plant dumps millions of gallons of treated sewage a day into the creek which runs past their homes.
>
> *Now* Bronson, Scott and other residents want the local water authority to do something about it...

Overlooking the awkward repetition of *do something about it,* which rather negates the work done by *and* and *now* in smoothing the story's flow, there is nothing much wrong with the use of *and* and *now* here.

But both these useful little words become tedious when over-employed. If the story eats *ands* and *nows* as a worn-out engine eats lubricating oil, try an overhaul.

The asthmatic comma

It is not the function of the comma to help a wheezing sentence get its breath back. That, however, is how the comma earns much of its living in daily journalism.

> Holidaymakers, who turned up in their hundreds to watch the sizzling sequel to their neck-and-neck first round 64s, saw Gallacher jet away with it.

Neither of those commas should be there – except that the sentence would turn purple in the face without them. Moreover, by demoting the arrival of the holidaymakers to a subordinate clause, they subtly promise a more exciting ending to the sentence than we are about to get.

The semi-colon, too, is often used as a breathing apparatus. In the following example, semi-colons have applied the kiss of life – and failed:

> When a group of children appear who are five times as likely to go to university as the national average; and when it turns out that all their mothers received a certain type of medical treatment before the children were born; doctors sit up and take notice.

This is wildly wrong. Semi-colons simply cannot be used as souped-up commas in this way. But even correct punctuation could not save this sentence. There is really nothing to do with it except demolish it and start again.

Here is how a healthy sentence can get by without either of these aids, so long as it keeps its nerve:

> Network operators and equipment manufacturers have been forced to pay considerably more attention to the needs and problems of the market place and customers growing increasingly restive at the quality and cost of services and pressing for more tailor-made rather than standard products.

The temptation to put a comma after *services* has been rightly resisted. It would have stopped the flow and obstructed the clarity of the sentence.

Here is what happens to an equally healthy passage, of shorter length, when it loses confidence in itself (or when someone handling the material has no confidence in it):

My father was a divorce barrister. When he came home from work he'd sit on the end of my bed and, instead of fairy stories, would give me accounts of his triumphs in the courts.

On the other hand, it is not unheard-of for an independent-minded sentence to refuse the help of a comma even when one is manifestly needed:

Torrential rain knocked out yesterday's racing at Epsom and a seven o'clock inspection this morning will decide if today's programme can go ahead.

Here we have two sentences masquerading as one, with the bridging *and* trying to bamboozle us into thinking that no punctuation is necessary. But it is. Until we near the end of this compendium sentence, we are being led to believe that torrential rain knocked out both the racing at Epsom and the seven o'clock inspection.

Moral: a sentence that obliges the reader to revise his opinion of what it is saying should be re-cast.

By and large, however, newspaper punctuation sins are those of commission rather than omission. There is a touching belief that bad construction can be cured by sprinkling the offending passage with commas:

Child-minders, are getting together to increase the number of toy libraries. Community-minded mothers are setting them up and, while children play and pick from the selection of toys unrestricted by the limits of family budgeting, their mothers, too, find companionship.

The comma after *child-minders* must be a literal: but in a piece with more commas that a roly-poly pudding has currants, it was probably overlooked. The comma after *setting them up and* is a gesture of despair: recognising that the construction is so awkward that it makes reading the passage a nasty experience for the reader, the comma does its futile best but then washes its hands of the entire sentence. Given the grotesque shape of the sentence, the remaining commas are appropriate – just as a steel brace would be appropriate for a twisted back. Taking the punctuation of this example as our criterion, let us see how another passage might have appeared in the *Daily Mirror*:

> At the end, after one of the most exciting FA Cup semi-finals I have ever seen, they trooped away, still quivering with the exhaustion that springs from unbearable tension, and unforgettable emotion.

Here is how it did appear – in the hands of a stylist:

> They trooped away at the end still quivering with the exhaustion that springs from unbearable tension and unforgettable emotion, after one of the most exciting FA Cup semi-finals I have ever seen.

The single comma, which is all this confident construction needs, not only does its basic job of clarification, it contributes towards the dramatic effect of the sentence. Elsewhere, the very *absence* of commas helps the rhythms that give this passage its air of excitement.

There is no space in this manual for a summary of the rules of punctuation, but a few random principles may be stated:

1. Many errors of punctuation are the result of carelessness rather than ignorance (see GRAMMAR). The basic rule of thumb 'If it feels right it probably is right' should serve those who have become a little hazy on the difference between a participial phrase and an absolute phrase. When in doubt, ask these questions: What is this comma/colon, semi-colon doing here? What is its job? Is the job being properly done, or is it just a bit of patchwork? Should the job be done by a punctuation mark at all, or is the comma/colon/semi-colon fulfilling the role of a six-inch nail supporting a badly fitting dovetail joint?

2. Beware the misplaced comma which distorts meaning, as in: 'Though to be fair, the Swedes defended stubbornly.' Nice of the Swedes to be fair in this way, the reader might think. If it was the reporter who wished to be fair, he would have needed an extra comma after *though*. Probably he could have borrowed one from a later sentence: 'It has to be stressed that this was a friendly match, in every sense of the word, with both sides allowing the midfield men room to work.' Which leads us to:

3. Commas are not condiments. Do not pepper sentences with them unnecessarily.

4. But they cannot be left out simply because they seem to be getting out of hand. 'On a blustery beach in the Channel Islands, Princess Caroline for so long the royal rebel of Monaco, is happy to step out of the limelight and romp with her three youngsters' requires one more comma after *Caroline*.

5. In newspapers, the colon's job of – to quote Fowler's delightful imagery – 'delivering the goods that have been invoiced in the preceding words' has been more or less handed over to the DOTS AND DASHES department. Its chief uses are to introduce a quote and to preamble a list or catalogue.

6. Once a series of semi-colons has been embarked upon, there can be no going back:

> Demanding curbs on the press, Labour's Bryan Gould calls for laws to split up big newspaper combines; to end foreign ownership; to give people unfairly attacked in the press the right to reply and controls on satellite TV.

There should be a semi-colon after *reply*. It has been left out either as superfluous or, more likely, because *controls* would then not be consistent with *to split, to end* and *to give*. But without the semi-colon, Labour is generously offering controls on satellite TV to people unfairly attacked in the press.

7. There is no general dispensation to do away with punctuation in headlines. HE AIN'T HEAVY HE'S TEETOTAL! requires a comma in the middle,

no matter in what size type it is set.

8. Never use punctuation marks to lend respectability to a sentence you would not otherwise care to introduce to your mother.

Captions

Caption-writing is a branch of literature that the tabloids have made all their own.

Where else, and in what other position than page three, could one read:

COR! KAREN PASSES HER OOH-LEVEL

Swot a stunner! Curvy Karen Brennan has blossomed from a cheeky-faced fourth-former into a classy 19-year-old.

As children return to their desks after the hols, Karen brushes up her French and thinks back to her schooldays.

The Bournemouth belle passed seven O-levels – and her Page Three Ooh-level exam.

– and the next question is, where else would one want to?

The caption-writer's problem is that he has no more than fifty or sixty words in which to say precisely nothing.

The only real information he starts out with is that his subject is a home-loving girl at heart, or that early birds at the Sussex seaside can glimpse jaunty Jane most mornings on her newly-bought bicycle, or that curvy Katie is a real pet when it comes to caring for animals. Neither the model's flat-decorating activities (which make her surroundings more attractive), nor her bicycle (which prevents her having a spare tyre), nor her cats (which help to keep her kittenish) usually figure in the picture – although when a Star Stunner did report to the studio with a kitten in her arms, the caption-writer was able to press it into service:

> Feline fancier Carol Needham would have been a natural for the role of Pussy Galore.
>
> She has two Persian moggies, Helmut and Jemima, and they have now been joined by another furry friend – this cute Burma kitten called Daisy.
>
> When she is not looking after her pets, Carol loves to visit the theatre. Her favourite show? Cats, of course!

Of course. But in general, the caption-writer is making bricks not only without straw but without clay. The best he can do is to embroider a mini-essay around the kind of arch small-talk heard from MCs of the Miss World contest when drawing it out of Miss Venezuela that she is fond of travel and makes many of her own dresses.

The jaunty caption goes back well into an era when the girls kept their clothes on. Fifty years ago, for some now obscure reason, nautical themes were much favoured, with *Show a leg there*! being a common intro. Although the pictures have changed with the times, the captions have made little progress. It is as if there has been an edict that this art form is as perfect as it ever will be, and that no further development is possible.

Certainly it must be difficult to write fifty attention-grabbing words when the subject of them is already engaging the reader's interest to the full and the only information required is not of the kind that appears in family newspapers. But that is no reason why the style of the caption should be set in aspic. After all, if back in those *Show a leg*! days it had been the fashion for captions to appear in rhyming couplets or as imaginary conversations between a ship's parrot and the first mate, someone would have demanded a change by now. There is no preservation order on the caption as an ancient monument, and the puns, *double entendres* and dated road-house expressions (heart-throb, dishy, nice little number) need not be part of the tabloid fabric for ever.

The *Daily Mirror*, indeed, has been known to

strike new ground by confining page three caption material (under, it has to be said, such headlines as THAT'S PRETTY, DEAR) to strictly utilitarian information on where such garments as the model might be wearing may be purchased, and for how much. In an even bolder experiment, a succession of page three Lucky Numbers linked with a bingo promotion dispensed with the daily dose of frothy wordplay altogether, merely noting, for example, that *Katie's in tip-top shape for a very important date – the launch of our new £20,000 bingo.* There was no evidence of a rush by the *Mirror* readership for the alternative page three of the *Sun* or the *Star*.

Page three captions that tie up lightheartedly with some general news event such as the weather, the Budget or the Cup Final (so long as the girl involved is not said to look like a winner who is gunning for Arsenal) are off to a better start than those that heartily simulate interest in the model's hobbies and aspirations. Away from the sway of curvy Karen and jaunty Jane, captions that have something to say should, of course, always win over those that do not, although this cannot be taken as a firm principle. *Halo, halo, what's going on here?* on a picture of an actor taking on the role of the Saint would do credit to any portrait of a curvy angel who has really been in heaven since her career took wings.

Catchwords

No pile-driver is any match for the popular press when it comes to driving a catchword into the ground.

Bonking (see SEX ROMPS) was at its height such a regular tabloid activity that the *Daily Star* and the *Sun* could have justifiably changed their names to the *Daily Bonk* and the *Bonk* respectively. Every day brought forth a new bonker – bonking Boris, a bonking bounder, a bonking grandpa, a bonking bishop – or new evidence of bonking in such headlines as BONKS A MILLION, BONKS FOR THE MEMORY and BONKS IN THE BANK. Then finally the *Sun,* introducing a new buzz-word which mercifully does not seem to have caught on, announced YUPPIES STOP BONKING AND START

PORKING! and the open season for bonking sputtered out. It will be a long time, however, before stray sightings of *bonk* cease to be reported.

Loadsamoney has had such a good run that if the comedian who coined the expression were on royalties he would be a millionaire by now – or *rolling in loadsadosh* as the tabloids would put it. There was a period when the simple term *money* virtually ceased to exist. Any reference to cash had to be in terms of *loadsamoney*. Then the partitive noun was detached from its host to give us *loadsa laughs, loadsa fellas, loadsa lovelies, loadsa Lawrie,* and *your loadsa-fun Sun,* offering *loadsamoney* in its bingo game. The *Sunday Times* had the headline LOADSA-SERMONS WON'T STOP THE THATCHERITE ROT, while its book review pages headed a notice of a book on popular capitalism with TEACHING THE LESSONS OF LOADSAMONEY.

Catchwords and catch-phrases – *lorra lolly, nick nick, nice little earner, on yer bike* – will always catch on with newspapers. Some last longer than others. *Mrs Mopp*, the standard journalistic term for cleaning ladies, was a character in a wartime radio series. Reflecting a facet of the passing show as they do, they are an essential ingredient of the tabloids. But as with so many other elements that make up the character of our daily journalism, a little of them goes a long way. Permutations on *loadsa* and the like become tiresome very quickly. They also, if remorselessly overdone, rob the paper of another of its essential ingredients – the ability to surprise. If the headline is so predictable that a space could be left for the readers to fill it in for themselves, it is time to give the ubiquitous catchword a rest.

Clichés (standard)

The newspapers have enough clichés of their own manufacture without having to borrow those in general use. The following were spotted in the briefest of browses through one day's papers:

> Takes the biscuit
> Back to square one
> Stoops to conquer
> Morning after the night before
> One for the road
> Cold comfort
> Jobs for the boys
> Living in a dream world
> Sure as God made little apples
> Sauce for the goose
> Live now, pay later

Against the grain
Doctor in the house
The good news is... The bad news is...
Pull their socks up
Waiting game
Taste of her own medicine
Right royal
Coming home to roost

This is discounting PUNS based on clichés such as the heading LOSING STREAK on the tale of a runaway pig which saved its bacon.

Clichés should be avoided by writers in general because reach-me-down phraseology has no place in original prose. They should be avoided by journalists in particular because it is the tendency of clichés to generalize, approximate or distort. Having said which, let us now hear Fowler quoting J. A. Spender: 'The hardest-worked cliché is better than the phrase that fails... Journalese results from the efforts of the non-literary mind to discover alternatives for the obvious where none are necessary...' Which leads us to:

Clichés (trade)

When Sam Goldwyn advised that clichés should be avoided like the plague, he forgot that the plague, by its very nature, is almost impossible to avoid. That is what gave the Black Death such a bad name.

Journalism has been contaminated by clichés since the profession began. It always will be. But not, mercifully, the same ones. Old clichés, like old soldiers, may not die but they do eventually fade away – to be replaced by new clichés.

Manuals of journalism published only a few years ago seem quaintly dated when they come to their lists of newspaper clichés – *burning issue, beggars description, like rats in a trap, limped into port, news leaked out, fair sex, speculation was rife,* and so on.

Most phrases of such antiquity would not be given house-room in a modern newspaper. But when we notice what *is* given house-room, it is evident that the cliché plague is not only still with us but that it is all the time developing powerful new strains resistant to any known antidote.

The day will never arrive when newspapers are cliché-free, but the following cross-section of words and phrases could vanish at once without any great loss to journalism. (Some of the examples in this selective, very incomplete list have been touched on elsewhere in these pages, but it will do no harm to touch on them again. One or two of them, like *knickers in a twist,* are or were in general use but have been appropriated by the newspapers.

And that's official
Angels (for nurses)
At the centre of a
  bitter row
Axed
Belt up (car
  seatbelts)
Billy Bunters
Boffins
Bonanza
Boost
Breakthrough
Caged (imprisoned)
Career girl
Cheeky
Clampdown
Cocktail of drugs
Crackdown
Cuppa
Curvy
Dashing
Death toll
Dishy
Down on the farm
Dream holiday
Dropped a clanger
Drugs hell
Fair cop
Fairytale ending
Fashion stakes
Feathers really flew

Flushed with shame
Getaway car
Glamour model
Giantkillers
Good buys
Hammered
Heartbreak mum
Heart-throb
Hello sailor
Helluva
High Street banks
Hurtle
Key role
Kiss 'n' tell
Knickers in a twist
Live-in lover
Love-child
Love rival/ cheat/
  split
Manhunt
Massive
Mercy dash
Merry widow
Nationwide
  hunt/search
Never-never land
Petite
Pinta
Pooch
Purrfect
Rampage

Rapped
Romeo vicar
Screen hunk
Sex kitten/bomb/
 beast
Sin-bin
Sir (for teachers)
Slammed
Slapped a ban
Soap queen
Soccer clash
Spree
Star-studded
Storm of opposition
Streets of fear

Stunned
Supremo
Sweet smell of
 success
There's an awful lot
 of coffee
Toyboy
Tragedy struck
Trouble flared
Vice queen
Village of fear
Vivacious
WAG
Whizzkid
Writing on the wall

And, of course, we must not forget the extras in this imposing cast of clichés: firemen, *many of them wearing breathing apparatus*, housewives, *many of them pushing prams* or *many of them carrying shopping bags*, and policemen, *many of them wearing riot gear*.

NOTE: In an era of radical change, clichés are now vulnerable not only to old age but to technological and social progress. *Gymslip mums*, for example, must have given way to *jeans and T-shirt mums* by now, while today's *carbon-copy deaths* are surely *photocopies*. Journalists who were not even born when businessmen last called their secretaries by their second names are still beginning stories with an office theme 'Take a letter, Miss Smith.'

Compression

Touching again on the original definition of tabloid journalism – *news in a concentrated form* – it is possible to overdo the compression.

This news in a concentrated form is from the *Daily Star:*

LEFTIES COMIC CAPERS

Loony lefties have torn a strip off kids' comics. They say the *Whizzer* and *Chips* and Enid Blyton's *Famous Five* adventure magazine are sexist. The *Eagle* is too macho and *Girl Monthly* 'totally offensive'.

Soccer hero Roy of the Rovers gets the boot for not having enough black team-mates. And the

Beezer is branded 'racist'. Among the few comics to find favour are the *Beano* and *Dandy*. They'll join *Lesbian and Gay Socialist* and *Spare Rib* on Camden Council's library shelves. A spokesman said: 'It's not a hard and fast guide.'

There the story ends, leaving the following questions unanswered:

What isn't a hard and fast guide?

For whom did the spokesman speak?

Who are these 'loony lefties'?

Why do they speak in the present tense about several publications known to be defunct?

Are we to take it from *Roy of the Rovers gets the boot* that some publications are banned while others are merely *branded*?

Why are *Beano* and *Dandy* to join *Lesbian and Gay Socialist,* etc. on the library shelves?

It is all too easy to sub down a story to the satisfaction of the chief sub who wants it in four inches, but to the bemusement of the reader. If this applies less to the text papers than to the tabloids it is only because they have more space. No story, whatever its ultimate length, should start life with the assumption that the reader will know what it is talking about.

Consequences

Probably few practitioners of modern journalism realize that the ground-rules for the narrative or human-interest story peculiar to popular newspapers ('It was gnash, fang, gollop, the day Gilbert the Pyrenean mountain dog tried to escape from a locked car...') were laid down in *Cassell's Book of Indoor Amusements, Card Games and Fireside Fun* in the year 1881.

The time-honoured game from which the rules derive is 'Consequences'. Its method of play – a formal sequence of adjectives, names, places, happenings and statements (or quotes), followed by 'the consequence' and 'what the world said' – is

remarkably similar to the way perhaps nir
ten human-interest stories are structured.

The classic opening for Fleet Street's
game is a short summary of *what resulted* ('It was one
darn thing after another') followed by *when* ('the
day' or 'the night') followed by *adjectives and name*
('27-stone Bessie Bottomley') followed by *event* ('lost
her knitting needles') followed by *where* ('in a
superstore's ladies' loo').

The narrative then proceeds chronologically, each
step being strictly governed by a preposition or
conjunction such as *for, and, but, so*:

For (expands on what resulted: Bulging Bessie
puts plump finger down drain and gets stuck);

And (continues to expand on what resulted: only
way she can get free is by ripping sink off wall);

But (new development promised: Bessie's heart
sinks – or blood *drains* from face – when she is
stopped by store detectives);

For (new development takes place: Bessie goes
round bend when arrested for shoplifting sink);

So (and the consequence was: Bessie's court
appearance, still with sink stuck on finger);

And (and the world said: quotes from magistrate,
Bessie and department store spokesman).

'Consequences' is a harmless game unless (as
often happens) it is played three or four times in the
same issue, when its deficiencies as a modern indoor
amusement or piece of fireside fun become apparent.
Its structure – with the obligatory *ands* and *buts* and
fors corseting the narrative like iron girders – is

altogether too rigid for a type of story that ought to bounce and bubble along. Moreover, the predestined, step-by-step approach often drags the story out beyond its natural length.

The chronological narrative may be the best way of telling a human-interest story, but that doesn't limit the storyteller to a particular style. Journalism has no especial commitment to the set 'Consequences' opening, which although it usually succeeds in grabbing the reader's interest then invariably leads him along the well-trodden *for-and-but-so* path.

'Consequences' should be played much more sparingly – and it should not be played at all when the game cannot be followed through:

> Villagers felt sore when the gun-slinging dentist went on the rampage.
>
> There was a fearsome gnashing of teeth as shots rang out from his garden.
>
> And sometimes the dentist, Peter Worledge, shot his mouth off – swearing at the villagers.
>
> But yesterday the armed gunman was rounded up for causing 'fear and annoyance'.
>
> He told a court that he would keep the peace for a year in the village of Hazlingfield, Cambridgeshire.
>
> Magistrates at Melbourn heard that Mr Worledge often fired his shotgun. But the worst time was one Sunday when his neighbour was chopping wood...

At this point it dawns on us that the narrative we

have just read was not a true narrative at all, but simply an elaborate preamble consisting of selected highlights from the gun-slinging dentist's saga, which now commences in earnest and goes on for another four paragraphs, in the course of which it repeats everything we have already been told. The game of 'Consequences' has become the game of 'Chinese Whispers'.

Crossheads

Crossheads, those stray words set in black type and often underlined which break up the column, go back to an era when newspapers had titles like the *Sporting and Police Gazette* or *Lloyd's Weekly News.* They were introduced to give the reader, and very likely the printer, periodic relief from eyestrain induced by endless tracts of tiny blurred type devoted to 'Extraordinary Charge of Drugging and Violence' and such matters. The crosshead was then a primitive device (it still is). It consisted merely of a few words of copy, usually in body-type and always integral to the text, centred and leaded where they fell into the story. Since the crossheads could not have been omitted without damaging the narrative, they could at least be said to have earned their keep.

With improved typography and the development of newspaper make-up, the device became more ornamental than functional. Had the crosshead not existed, tabloid newspapers in particular would have had no need to invent it.

It is all the more remarkable, therefore, that it is only in the tabloids that the crosshead continues to flourish. On a day taken at random [in 1989], the *Daily Mirror, Daily Star* and *Sun*, all with 32 pages, had respectively 18, 45 and 34 crossheads (although it has to be said that the *Sun*'s total was 30 less than when first monitored by this manual ten years earlier). The *Daily Mail*, with 40 pages, had 43, the

Express, also with 40 pages, had 33, while the 36-page *Today* had 38.

Yet the broadsheet *Times, Guardian, Independent* and *Daily Telegraph* sported not a single crosshead between them.

There is something absurd about spattering a page not much bigger than a sheet of A4 with odd words apparently picked from the dictionary with a pin. (It is even more absurd when the paragraph to which the crosshead refers has been cut out on the stone, as often happens.) *Wait, Bonus, Roses, Frosty, Sorry* are from the *Sun*'s bumper crop mentioned above: none of them informs the reader or tempts him to read on. The *Star's Pyjamas, Planned, Cleavage, Disgust, Dirty looks*, do at least draw lip-smacking attention to the bedroom revelations they adorn.

The broadsheets, and the tabloids themselves on occasion (particularly the *Daily Mirror*), have shown that a newspaper can get by virtually without these cryptic aids, especially in features material where there is an abundance of alternatives (which need not necessarily be THE INCREDIBLE BLOB) available.

Where crossheads are deemed to be necessary, however, they are worth more attention than they sometimes get. The standard crosshead consists of one word, usually of no more than seven or eight characters. The temptation is to assume that any old word will do. It will not (although the *News of the World*, in a story about THE MOST BORING MAN IN BRITAIN, had fun peppering it with crossheads that had no relevance at all to the text, though they were relevant to its subject: *Waffle, Piffle, Snore* and *Ho-hum*). Every word that gets into print should have something to say. Crossheads need not be the exception.

Abstract nouns that relate to human behaviour (*Sorrow, Theft, Attack*) are better than abstract nouns that don't (*Role, Magic, Nights)* and infinitely better than most concrete nouns (*Table, Coach, Lamp*).

But verbs or adjectives may be better still. *Stole* is better than *Theft*, night lawyers allowing, and *Hot* is better than *Heat*.

A set of crossheads shouldn't stray from one word-class to another – from a noun to a verb to an adjective, for example. *Sorrow, Stole, Hot* has no logic, and is therefore vaguely disturbing even though the reader can't spot what's amiss.

Sometimes – in features rather than news stories – the chance comes up to brush a set of crossheads with a little wit. Alliteration (*Hot, Hazy, High*), word-association (*Faith, Hope, Charity*), comparatives (*Good, Better, Best*) and suchlike harmless indulgences may not be in the Stone-sub of the Year Award class, but they are an improvement on *Wait, Bonus, Roses,* etc.

Titillating crossheads that do not fulfil their promise – *Whips*, when scrutiny of the body-type reveals a harmless reference to the House of Commons voting arrangement – are best left to the successors to the *Sporting and Police Gazette* and *Lloyd's Weekly News.* Which is where we came in.

Dead letters

Journalists with flair write in the language of their readers. Readers with even more flair write in the language of their newspapers.

> Supermarket checkout girl Julie Burns, 19, deserved praise not the sack after reporting two louts who paid only £25 for goods worth £56 and warned her: 'Tell anyone and we'll carve you up.'
>
> Manager Tom Kelly behaved callously in dismissing Julie at the Victor Value store in Huyton, Liverpool...

Or could that letter to the *Daily Mirror* possibly have passed through the hands of a sub-editor?

Of course letters to the editor cannot be printed

exactly as they are written – at any rate, not in the tabloids. Readers with little education tend to be rambling and repetitive. They also have their own repertoire of tired phrases – *why oh why, mere housewife, made my blood boil,* etc. On the other hand, their letters are often fresh and invigorating. They probably need tidying up a little but it is a shame to sub all the life out of them by re-writing them in a wooden style which the sub-editor would not dream of using of he were writing home to his mother.

Every letters page editor is familiar with the compulsive correspondent who daily bombards the newspapers with pithy letters on every conceivable subject. Their trademark is that they are written in excruciating imitation of tabloid English at its most mechanical. These readers really do write letters beginning 'I'm not sorry Hole In The Wall, hosted by Anton Du Beke, has been axed...' Rightly, these offerings are usually spiked. The sub-editor then reaches for a genuine letter on the same subject and proceeds to rewrite it in the same dead style.

Readers' letters should read like readers' letters. They should not reveal signs of heavy editorial compression or re-working (usually most evident in the obligatory summary of the topic under discussion: 'I'm amazed at reader Mrs I. Horner's narrow-minded view that motor sports should be banned...')

Home-grown hackneyed phrases of the *made my blood boil* variety should by all means be excised. Nor should the readers' letters column be a sanctuary for awkward English: 'How unfortunate to have so little sense of humour as the recent reader who saw nothing to laugh at in ITV's In Loving Memory.'

A recent reader is one who is not long past. Most newspapers would prefer to have their readers living in the present.

Dots and dashes

Two news items. Same day, same paper, same page:

> Kids today have a driving ambition – and it's NOT with British Rail...

> Florists stole wreaths and flowers after funerals... then sold them for a second time to other mourners...

Had the journalist handling the first story handled the second, and vice versa, they could very well have read:

> Kids today have a driving ambition... and it's NOT with British Rail...

> Florists stole wreaths and flowers after funerals – then sold them for a second time to other mourners...

Dots and dashes, in Fleet Street if not in the fastidious world outside, are regarded as interchangeable. That suggests there is some vagueness about how they ought to be used.

These are some of the proper uses of dots:

1. Where a sentence tails off because the ending of it is already familiar to the reader, as in *A fool and his money...*

2. Where the writer wants to suggest that there is more that could be said on the subject, as in *But that's another story...*

3. Where a sub-deck, like the verse of a song, leads into the chorus-headline, as *Thanks to the lads...* WE'RE HOME.

4. Where (usually in a quotation) some words have been omitted, as in *This brilliant play... should run and run and run.*

5. Where a quotation is not completed, as in most of the examples given here.

These are some of the improper uses of dots:

1. Where the dots should be a dash, as in:

> Stand by for the best Easter present of all... some bright weather to shoo away those winter blues...

2. Where the dots should be a comma:

> A teenage girl lies dead on the

pavement… the victim of a savage knife attack yesterday on her way to work…

3. Where the dots are in effect saying 'Wait for it' before the chortling pay-off is delivered, as in *The lovesick dentist's dowry to his bride was…* (wait for it) *a mouthful of gold teeth.* (Where we have to wait for it, it is worth asking whether it's worth waiting for.)

4. Where the dots are simply added as makeweight to a headline that is too short. (FAREWELL MY LOVELY, if it didn't quite fit, could well read FAREWELL MY LOVELY…)

Some of the proper uses of dashes:

1. As above, where dots have been wrongly used.

2. As parentheses, as in *Later – speaking at Heathrow – Mrs Thatcher said…*

3. In headlines, as attribution, as in LET BOMBERS HANG – POLICE.

4. As an additional, surprising twist to the sentence, as in *Train fares look certain to rise again this summer – despite British Rail's £58m profit last year.*

Some improper uses of dashes:

1. The dash standing in for missing words:

> The court at Slough, Berks, heard that the Colonel had a string of glamorous lady friends – and installed his favourites in palatial houses.

The mystery of why the court should want to do this expensive favour for the Colonel is cleared up when we realize that the dash, in combination with the *and,* is doing service for *and that he.* This is no part of a dash's job.

2. Dashes standing in for commas: *Mr Smith – who was last year's committee chairman – will head the inquiry.* The dashes are here used as parentheses, but the sense calls for commas rather than brackets. But in JOURNALESE, *Mr Smith – he was last year's committee chairman – will head the inquiry* is acceptable.

3. One dash trying to do the job of two: *Ben Johnson – without his gold medal, flew home in disgrace last night.* This requires either two dashes or two commas, but not one of each. The dash opens brackets; it needs another dash to close them.

4. Finally, and studiously ignoring the dangerously high pun-content (see PUNS AND WORDPLAY) in the following story, the dash that doesn't know what it is doing:

> Shaggy sailor John Holmes was cut to the quick by his shipmates. They called him Veronica because of his long hair. But the unkindest cut of all for John was when an officer picked up the scissors – and went scalp-hunting on the good ship Mohawk.

The dash, if it has any purpose at all, is a punctuation mark. Punctuation is among other things about pauses. There is absolutely no reason to pause in the above passage, since the effect that could have been made by pausing is spoilt by the words going on for longer than they should. *Picked up the scissors – and went scalp-hunting* would have been all right within the lights of this story. *Picked up the scissors – and went scalp-hunting on the good ship* Mohawk goes on a beat too long. Moral: if you don't know where to stop, don't start.

Dramatic events drama

If a news story is dramatic, the drama should come out of the telling. It is not enough simply to assure readers that the drama was there. Such phrases as *dramatic dash, took a dramatic turn,* etc. in the text, or DASH DRAMA in the headline, are no more than labels to let the reader know what type of story he is reading. They do not convey the drama to him – any more than *funny walk, took a funny turn* or DASH JOKE would make him laugh.

By the same token, *colourful* places and characters should be seen to be colourful, not just asserted as such.

Facetiousness

Several of the examples quoted below would be equally at home in PUNS AND WORDPLAY (which should be read in conjunction with this entry). The pun, however, is as essential an ingredient of facetiousness as sugar is of candy-floss, and so some overlapping is inevitable.

What is facetiousness in newspapers, and what is it for? The most accurate definition is probably that it is a form of sustained banter. It joshes the reader from sentence to sentence, rather like an old-fashioned club comedian. (An amusing way of whiling away a dull morning is to go through the worst of the day's crop of facetious stories, interpolating such expressions as ''Ere, lady!', 'It's true!', 'Listen, missus!', 'He did it, honest!' and so on between paragraphs.)

As to its purpose, this probably stems from the deep-seated fear of a once-secure profession that its readers would probably rather be watching soap operas than reading their newspapers. The object is to be entertaining *at all costs*. The story should be effortless to read, which means it must look as if it was effortless to write. Such, anyway, is the theory. In fact the facetious story is as often as not the kind of soufflé that could be used as a doorstop.

The following 'story' accompanied two pictures of the Boat Race teams – Cambridge conventionally clad, Oxford stripped to the waist:

A CHEEKY STROKE FOR THE BIG RACE

The husky oarsmen of Oxford, bidding for four Boat Race wins in a row, stole a cheeky march on their rivals yesterday.

They were determined to give Cambridge plenty to beef about before today's race.

So after a hectic gym work-out, they showed what they're made of… by baring their chests and setting their muscles a-rippling.

The power parade made quite a splash – especially with the Dark Blues' young female fans.

But Cambridge decided to play it cool.

They posed sedately for pre-race pictures… and then quietly planned how to pull the plug on their opponents between Putney and Mortlake.

If they succeed it will be an upset.

For Oxford are already 6-4 on favourites to coast home for their first four-in-a-row since 1912.

In less than 140 words, this item has managed to incorporate just about every fault and flaw in popular journalism discussed in these pages.

As a newspaper report, this extreme example is, of course, 95 per cent padding. In twenty-six lines of type, half of them double-column, it contains one new fact (the betting odds). It contains two old facts from Whittaker's Almanack (Oxford has won three in a row; last four in a row was in 1912). The rest of the story simply consists of words loosely evocative of Boat Races that happen to have been put together in this particular order, but which could have been put in any other order and still made as much sense – which is to say, not much sense at all.

The story is not so much written as assembled. It is a collage of clichés (*stole a march, play it cool*), puns and *double entendres* (*plenty to beef about, showed what they're made of, quite a splash, pull the plug out*), and slot-machine adjectives (*husky, hectic*), all bound together with antiquated Fleet Street verbiage, including the venerable *Dark Blues' young female fans*.

It is clear that some unfortunate journalist was here given the task of making something out of nothing. It can be stated as a principle that the less there is in a story, the higher its facetiousness content.

When the actress Penelope Keith first appeared in *Who's Who* she gave her hobby as gardening. Is this news item, here summarized in 16 words, worth 110 more? Here – to adapt Parkinson's Law – is how the story expands to fill the space allocated:

I say, how splendid. The world's worst snob, Margo Leadbetter, has finally reached the top of the tree.

Her nibs Penelope Keith, the actress who played snooty Margo in BBC-TV's 'The Good Life', has received the ultimate accolade for social graces.

She joins the rest of the nation's upper crust in the latest issue of *Who's Who*.

The top people's directory lists Penelope's hobby as... GARDENING – a subject even Margo would have approved of.

But last night the former convent girl Penelope, 37, was keeping a dignified silence over her inclusion in Who's Who.

A family friend said: 'Margo would be jolly pleased. It would be one over Mrs Whatsername at the operatic society.

'But I can't speak for Penelope. She is more modest than Margo...'

And so on. It will be noted that we are more than a quarter into this typographical fortune cookie before its slender message is revealed, and that the only development after that is the conjecture of a 'family friend' on the possible reaction of a fictitious character in a TV sitcom.

We have looked at stories that contain facetiousness and little else, as a balloon contains air. The technique is often used in stories that could well stand up without it:

Sparkling news, chaps! Uncork a bottle and raise your glasses to the vintage years ahead.

If your favourite tipple is wine, your health prospects are healthy. But for goodness sake lay off the hard stuff.

Experts have discovered that wine – a little of which has always been good for the stomach – can also ease the strain on the heart.

A team from the Medical Research Council studied the drinking habits of eighteen countries.

And they report in the *Lancet* journal that the more wine a nation drinks, the lower the death rate from heart disease among middle-aged men...

A sensation of *déjà vu* would be understandable at this point. A feature of stories written in this style is that the news has to be presented twice – the funny version followed by the more or less straight version.

Without the same generous allocation of space at our disposal, it is time to bring these examples to an end and summarize the case against facetiousness:

1. Sustained facetiousness is evidence of warped editorial judgement. It is right that stories should be allocated space and prominence according to their potential reader-interest, but that should not be the only yardstick. Where it is the only yardstick, and no judgement is made on the treatment, quality or content of the story, then the paper is bound to find itself devoting valuable column inches to potential and nothing else. In other words, it is printing the

shopping list instead of delivering the goods – as in the *Who's Who* story, which might be worth eight inches with some good quotes from Penelope Keith, yet still gets eight inches without any quotes from her at all.

2. If proper editorial judgement is not used, then facetiousness will flourish and there will always be a market for it. Professional journalists will always tailor their material to the market. The demand for the product therefore creates the kind of cynical outlook embraced by the disclaimer, 'This is what they want, this is what they'll get.'

3. Facetious writing is nothing more that padding or verbiage. The only case ever made out for padding in journalism ceased to be valid when newspapers stopped paying their contributors at the rate of a penny a line.

4. Facetiousness is not witty, for all that a well-honed pun may cause mock groans of appreciation among readers as far away from Fleet Street as Ludgate Circus. It is not intellectually clever. It is a mechanical trick. In extreme cases, it can become the verbal equivalent of a nervous tic. It is also very irritating to onlookers. Like children obsessively droning 'Wall, tall, fall, call, small, ball, hall,' its perpetrators must finally reduce their audience to fury.

5. Soft-core pornography is supposed to encourage a taste for hard-core pornography. Here the process is reversed. Hard-core facetiousness encourages soft-core facetiousness. It will, unless

checked, ultimately sweep through the paper like elm-blight. To a great extent it is doing so already, for pieces that are not, overall, written in the facetious style may often be found to be tainted with facetiousness. The penultimate example in this section will serve as an illustration of this tendency.

The *Daily Mirror* ran a short news story about the owner of a celebrated talking dog being plagued by obscene phone calls. In the headline he was inevitably *hounded* and in the intro he was inevitably being *dogged*, but apart from these initial aberrations the report was straightforward enough. It was an interesting little story that did not need any window-dressing. In the last paragraph, however, after we had been told that the Post Office are now intercepting calls, the dog owner is quoted as saying, 'They'll all be barking up the wrong tree now.'

This statement, in its context, makes no sense at all. It might just as well have read, 'I feel like a glass of water', or 'A good cigar is a smoke.' The only excuse for using it is that the old saw about barking up wrong trees is connected with dogs, and the story is about dogs. That, in the fantasy world of facetiousness, is enough.

There is one more aspect of this wearisome style that must be touched upon.

The flippant, facile approach is doubly reprehensible when it is inappropriate to the subject. It is easy, by allowing the narrative to run on the familiar, stereotyped, jocular lines, to appear indifferent or even callous towards the actual human being involved in the 'human story'.

EYES-UP FOR A DISASTER

> Bingo fans knew that trouble was on the cards when Margaret Fieldhouse suddenly dropped in.
>
> For Margaret, 46, made her unexpected entrance *through the ceiling.*
>
> A full house of 300 bingo players stared up in astonishment as her legs came crashing through the plaster...

The temptation to lay on the bingo terms thick has been resisted. Paragraph three could easily have read: *It was a case of eyes up for a full house when Bingo! LEGS ELEVEN! Margaret's legs came crashing through the top of the shop...*

Despite this admirable restraint, the story for half its length is told in the standard facetious manner. Given the editorial demand for this kind of thing, the flip approach seems justified. After all, falling through a ceiling can – conceivably – be funny. It is the stuff of slapstick.

But in banana-skin comedy, nobody really gets hurt. When somebody does really get hurt, it ceases to be comedy. It is therefore necessary, in the second half of this story, to straighten the editorial face before continuing:

> Last night, after treatment for a broken leg and injured spine, she was back home in Logwood Close, Wigan, Lancs.
>
> Margaret, who works as a cashier in a cinema

above the bingo hall in Wigan, was too upset to talk.

Perhaps the lady had a good laugh when she read about her mishap in the tabloids.

Free Speech

Much of the reported speech in the news columns could be filed under the heading of what the *New Yorker* calls 'Quotes we doubt ever got quoted'.

A common technique is to put the reporter's question into the mouth of the interviewee, so that the answer 'Certainly not' expands to read, 'Did I visit sleazy clubs and have sex romps with topless hostesses, one of whom was only sixteen and younger than my daughter? Certainly not.'

Then there is the protracted, usually paid for, exclusive interview quote, also very often on the SEX ROMPS theme: 'After visiting a swish Mayfair club where he plied me with drinks, I was whisked home in his red Porsche to the luxury flat I was renting out of my £1,000-a-week earnings...' She may have signed it, but she didn't say it.

Another school of thought goes on the excellent principle that eye-witness accounts are the best but they always seem to turn out like an interview with another reporter: 'There was a terrific explosion, then people began falling like dominoes. Firemen were quickly on the scene but they had to battle against clouds of thick black smoke...'

Despite the invention of the tape recorder, many newspapers have a tin ear for dialogue. The *San Francisco Chronicle* carried this alleged quote from an English couple in a story about a ferry strike: 'This is a lousy break for us, because we're here from England and we were told the ferry was a great treat. It's just too bad because we're headed for Los Angeles this afternoon and I guess we won't have a chance to ride the boat.'

Real people do not talk like journalists or like girlie magazines or as if they were giving evidence at an inquest or making a statement to the police. They talk as one hears them talking in radio and TV interviews. The discrepancy shows.

Even when quotes yield strictly facts rather than impressions, they should have the feel of someone speaking rather than someone writing.

But the public, like the press, has an extensive repertoire of phrases that have seen better days: *It was like Aladdin's cave in there... I'm over the moon... worse than the Blitz... they were like animals... sick as a parrot... not good enough... driving like maniacs...*

winter of discontent... I was sickened... never had a chance... saw this ball of fire coming towards us...

Stereotyped speech is to be avoided as much as stereotyped reportage.

Grammar

Most journalists, like most other people, have forgotten all they were ever taught about gerunds, dative cases, present subjunctives and so forth. Fortunately, they have usually retained a grasp of syntax which has become almost instinctive – but with some blind spots.

A few blots from Fleet Street's copybook (errors italicized, explanations parenthesized):

As Britain's first Minister for Sport, *no one* did more at all levels to help British sport. (Unless we are sneaking in a political judgement here, we cannot really claim that the Minister for Sport was nobody.)

If you have something to laugh at, complain about, *or an experience to share,* the *Mirror* wants to hear it. (The catalogue is governed by *something to,* which requires verbs. *An experience* is not a verb. But the insertion of *or* in place of the comma between *laugh at* and *complain* would have restricted the catalogue to those two items, and *or an experience* would then have been in order.)

The comedy team discuss one another, one another's legs, dentistry, stomach complaints, hair transplants, and *throw food at the camera.* (The catalogue is governed by *discuss* which requires nouns. *Throw* is not a noun. But the insertion of *and* between *complaints* and *hair transplants* could have brought the passage to an end before the offending passage.)

We would *kindly* ask that readers who wish to contribute to this column should phone a special number. (Nice of the *Daily Mail* to ask, but the kindliness is on the part of the readers, not the paper.)

According to a *Sunday Mirror* survey of more than 1,000 mums and dads, they are perfectly aware that many of these youngsters do things like: *stay* out late at night at discos, *spend* their evenings in pubs, *drink* alcohol… (They do things like *staying* out, *spending* their evenings at pubs, etc.)

It's *us* who dread Saturday evenings. (It's *we* who dread writing like this in the *Telegraph* magazine.)

Races are not particularly exciting for most women, unless *she's* one of those who like to pose around the track. (These singular women appear by courtesy of James Hunt.)

By simply showing your baby groups of dots on cards every day *he will quickly learn to identify the total number of dots.* (Either half of the sentence could be italicized as the error. The person of the first part should be the person of the second part also.)

Looking at these examples, few would be able to say without reference to an elementary English grammar that the reason Britain's Minister for Sport appears to be Mr Nobody, and the baby seems to be showing itself groups of dots, is that the participial phrase does not refer to the grammatical subject. But it should be plain to most journalists that there is something wrong with the construction. Where grammatical errors do occur, carelessness or haste rather than blissful ignorance is usually to blame.

In general, if a sentence feels right, it probably is right. If it seems awkward, then it needs investigation. Where the writer's ear tells him he may be on grammatically shaky ground but he cannot remember the particular rule of grammar that would rescue him, it is often possible to find out what, if anything, is wrong by applying simple tests. Some examples:

Should it be *who* or *whom*? Substitute *he* for *who* or *him* for *whom*, if necessary juggling the words around to accommodate the substitution. *I did not know HE was the editor* is correct, so *I did not know* WHOM *was the editor is* incorrect. *Should I get my expenses from HE?* is incorrect, so *From* WHOM *should I get my expenses?* is correct. (This should dispose of the genteel idea that *whom* is merely *who* with its little finger sticking out.

Should it be *he and I* or *him and me*? Try leaving one pronoun or the other out of the sentence for a moment. *Will you meet I?* is obviously wrong. *Will you meet HIM?* is obviously right. So *Will you meet HIM AND ME?* would be the correct form.

Should it be *us* or *we*? Omit the noun that belongs to the *us* or *we* pronoun and see what happens. *Only the lunatic few among WE did not condemn Brian Rose's one-run declaration* doesn't sound right, so it should be *Only the lunatic few among US Somerset members did not condemn...* Where the pronoun is not accompanied by its noun, try adding the repeated verb that is implicitly there. *They are no better than US ARE* can't be correct, so *They are no better than WE* is correct.

Should it be *is* or *are?* Straightforward plurals (*ships and shoes and carpenters*) are easy to handle, but what about when they are not straightforward, and may not be plurals? *A ship, a shoe and a carpenter ARE among exhibits in the Lewis Carroll Museum* sounds right, and is right. (Number of things among exhibits: three. Therefore plural.) *A ship, a shoe or a carpenter IS to be among the exhibits* sounds doubtful, but is still right. (Number of things that will go into the museum: one. Therefore singular.) Further explorations in the *is/are* jungle are unwise without a guide. But two basic rules are:

1. In *neither-nor* or *either-or* sentences, the verb matches the nearest subject. (*Neither the ship, nor the shoe, nor the carpenter IS among the exhibits.* But: *Neither the ship, nor the other things mentioned, ARE among the exhibits.*

2. But without the *nor/or*, *neither/either* takes the singular verb, as do *everyone, someone, everybody, nobody, each,* etc. (*Although the ship is among the exhibits, neither of the other two things IS.*)

Should it be *compare with* or *compare to?* It depends on what the *compare* sentence is doing. If the idea is to put one thing in the same class as another, then *compare to* would be right. *He COMPARED me TO Shakespeare* (i.e., to my advantage). But if the idea is to show that one thing is *not* in the same class as another, in other words to set up a comparison, then *compare with*: HE COMPARED *me* WITH *Shakespeare* (i.e., to my detriment).

But all these are rules of thumb, and thumbs have a reputation for sticking out when sore. If being 'correct' makes the sentence stiff at the joints, it may be better to be colloquial. Nor is there any point in ploddingly doctoring an 'incorrect' sentence in order to give it a clean bill of grammatical health. Either a sentence jars or it doesn't; if it does jar, the most sensible course is to reconstruct it altogether.

If a passage doesn't feel right, a good way of checking its grammatical credentials is by the Mission Impossible test:

> *He mixed with Prince Philip.* No, he couldn't have done. It takes a minimum of three to mix, and even then they are probably mingling.

> *She has made strong men weep – not just the members of the public at whom she preached and patronized...* Not possible. She could not have patronized *at* anybody.

> *Prince Charles stunned an audience of TV and film executives yesterday with a scathing attack over violence on the screen.* How does one go about *attacking over*?

Writing is very likely grammatically sound if on close scrutiny it still makes sense.

(Some other pitfalls are discussed under WHICH IS THAT?, THE NUMBERS GAME and THE ASTHMATIC COMMA.)

Great Minds

Great minds do not think alike. Great minds think differently.

The nearest examples to hand of Fleet Street telepathy:

1. A shopkeeper was blacked by 4,000 shipyard workers because she put a penny on the price of a cheese roll. The *Daily Star* reported: 'Her 18 pence rolls *cheesed off* a union boss.' The *Sun* reported: '*Cheesed off*... that's shopkeeper Christina Todd.' The *Daily Mirror* reported: 'Now granny Christina's business has slumped to nothing – leaving her really *cheesed off.*'

2. Headlines on an item about motorists causing accidents by looking up at an air show instead of keeping their eyes on the road:

Sun: PLANE CRAZY
Daily Star: PLANE CRAZY
Daily Mirror: PLANE CRAZY
Daily Express: PLANE CRAZY

3. When the chocolate firm of Rowntree's was the subject of a takeover bid, Fleet Street went to its headline slot machines which almost unanimously yielded BAR WARS.

4. 'Tote betting seems odds-on favourite for privatization' – *Daily Telegraph*.

'The people's bookie, the Tote, is odds-on favourite for privatization' – *Daily Express*.

5. The telepathic influence was strong on the day a man was taken to court for signing his electoral form 'Mr Kermit'.

The *Express* said that council officials were *hopping mad*.

The *Sun* said: 'Mr Kermit gets *hopping mad*.'

The *Daily Star* said: '*Kermit* went a-courting yesterday... and ended up *hopping mad*.'

But the *Daily Mirror* story began: 'Kermit the Frog hopped along to court yesterday', and then told how 'Doncaster council frog-marched him before local magistrates.'

It was funny and refreshing, and unlike the great thinking behind the *Express*, *Sun* and *Star* versions it didn't run on tram lines.

Moral: Think of the obvious, and then discard it. Or as the style book of a provincial daily quoted in the *UK Press Gazette* warns, 'Be suspicious of the story that seems to write itself, and of the phrase that comes to mind too readily.'

Worse than less-than-great minds thinking alike is the mind that thinks what has already been thought.

Whoever first put the headline THUGS BUNNY (a twist on the name of a Warner Brothers cartoon character, born 1936) on a picture of a tough-looking rabbit was an innovator.

Whoever did it next was a plagiarist.

Those who did it for the third, fourth, tenth, twentieth and hundredth times were stereotypists.

The same goes for such old chestnuts as CLOWN PRINCE, CATCH OF THE DAY and COSTA PACKET. Yet even when a headline has long been a stereotype, there is always room for one more ingenious twist. Thus, years after THUGS BUNNY, LUGS BUNNY, MUGS BUNNY, etc. had ceased to be clever, the *Mirror* looked at a picture of a rabbit fostering a kitten and headlined it BUGS MUMMY. That was original and funny.

NOTE: This dispensation does not apply to any variation on PHEW! WHAT A SCORCHER! (see THE WEATHER VANE

How say you?

Tick the correct tense:

'I have never seen anything like it. They were like animals,' *said* Mrs Smith.

'It is the same every Saturday night. They are like animals,' *says* Mrs Jones.

Both should be ticked. Both would be correct (but not in the same story).

Said is used when the witness or spokesman is describing a one-off incident – a fire, an accident, or perhaps (as in Mrs Smith's experience above) one of those disturbances known to Fleet Street as a *rampage.*

Says is used when the witness or spokesman is describing a constant or generality – something that is always pretty much the same, such as the Bank Holiday takings at the zoo or the traffic jams on the Chiswick flyover or the aforesaid Mrs Jones's neighbourhood every Saturday night.

Said, covering immediate events, is more often than not appropriate for news stories. *Says*, covering the background, is more likely to appear in a feature or back-up story.

Says may also appear in a feature interview. But when it does, the whole piece should be in the present tense, not only the quotes.

Whether in the present, past or future tense, avoid the inversion as in 'Claims Mrs Jones: "They urinate in the floral clock."' This style was popular many years ago when the *Daily Express* was imitating *Time* magazine, which then contained so many inversions that the *New Yorker* finally commented: 'Backward ran sentences until reeled the mind.' But it is old hat now.

Hyphens

What have these hyphenated words in common: *tough-guy, sight-seeing, hand-out, rat-pack, smoked-salmon, single-parent, baby-faced, funny-man, top-secret*?

The answer is that they were all in the same day's tabloids and that all their hyphens are unnecessary. *Tough guy, smoked salmon, single parent, top secret* look perfectly all right without a hyphen: *sightseeing, handout, ratpack, babyfaced, funnyman* read better as fusions.

The newspapers are as crammed with hyphens as a spotted dick (not spotted-dick) with currants. Many arise out of a fondness for prefixing names with descriptive nuggets of information like *fifteen-stone mother-of-three Eileen*, which is legitimate (so far as the hyphens are concerned). But the habit has become so ingrained that one can read in the *Sun* that the £800-a-day boss of Rover earns *a whopping £800-a-day,* which is a superfluity of hyphens, as is the Daily *Mail's one-in-eight drivers use unsafe tyres* (which incidentally should be *one in eight* uses *unsafe tyres*).

The main purpose of the hyphen is to marry two or three words so that they read as one: *mother-in-law, sixty-six, bust-up.*

Some of its other uses:

As in *Burma-Siam railway,* to stand in for the preposition *to.*

As in *man-made, custom-built, airy-fairy, African-born,* where the hyphen bridges two interdependent words.

As in *ice-cold, red-hot, grass-green,* where the hyphen links a description to what is being described.

As in *re-formed,* where a re-formed wine committee would otherwise be a reformed wine committee.

As in *attention-grabbing, mind-boggling* (but no longer, e.g., *bloodcurdling*), where a noun and a verb form an adjective; or *copy-edit* where a noun particularizes a verb.

As in *heart-throb, hitch-hike, co-operation,* where the hyphen keeps apart words which respectively end and begin with the same letter (although the Americans often fail to *cooperate* with this rule).

As in *40-a-day chain-smoker Peter,* or *Peter, a 40-a-*

day chain-smoker; or *three-times-married Susan* (but not *Susan, three-times-married*), where hyphens hold together a piece of information subsidiary to what the rest of the sentence is saying.

As in *three-year-old children*, where the meaning could be ambiguous without the hyphens. Three year old children could mean three children a year old.

As in *love-tug mum*, where an established tabloid compound is being used. It would be better if it were not, but if we have to have a love-tug mum, her dilemma ought to be hyphenated.

Hyphens should never be used when they have nothing to do. Before admitting one to the page, ask what it has come for. If it cannot say, or if the answer is vague – '*Shopping spree* just looks as if it ought to be *shopping-spree*' – refuse it admission.

Such hyphens as are allowed in should be checked for consistency. *Superstar* and *mega-star* on the same page, or even in the same paper, are inconsistent. If *superstar* doesn't need a hyphen (and it doesn't) then neither does *megastar*.

Hyphens have a welcome tendency to wither away *Housewife, fingerprints, railway, handbook,* are all examples of compounds which started life with hyphens. When it looks as if the time has come when a compound no longer needs a hyphen, then allow it to throw away its crutch.

Illiterals

Literals are typographical errors which somehow manage to get themselves blamed on the typography rather than on the typographer – or the journalist.

Many of them are in truth what we might call *illiterals*, born of ignorance rather than inefficiency. With the influence of that noble body the Correctors of the Press sadly on the wane, far more illiterals than ever are now getting into print. The fact that far more of them are also being perpetrated in the first place is probably due to the decline in education.

The commonest illiteral is the misplaced apostrophe, usually *it's* for *its*. All one need remember about apostrophes is that they are used to indicate the possessive (*the Pope's, St James's* [but not

St James'], *Mrs Thatcher's*) including the pronoun *one* (but *oneself*, if one word), but excluding all other pronouns (*its, hers, ours, theirs* – Tennyson was the last person authorized to write *Their's not to reason why*); that they must be kept well away from plurals (*potatoes, bananas, the Joneses*); but that the possessive of a plural is apostrophized after rather than before the possessive *s* (*the Joneses' place, ministers' responsibility, peoples'* if we are talking about the peoples of the world, otherwise as in *people's republic*).

Misplaced or missing commas are the next most common illiterals. They are dealt with under the heading of THE ASTHMATIC COMMA.

The not so singular practice of switching from the singular to the plural (*Today*'s royal correspondent in writing 'No mother could have tried harder to give their son a perfect fourth birthday' was presumably thinking of the royal we) and sundry other grammatical peccadilloes are also looked at elsewhere.

Factual errors are not really this manual's business unless they arise from bad or sloppy writing or careless copy-editing. They often do. When *Today* headlines a story beginning 'The nationwide boom in house process is showing signs of slowing down' with GOING DOWN! HOUSE PRICES ARE FALLING, it is misleading the reader either by misinterpreting its own story or by assuming that *going down* and *slowing down* are the same thing. They aren't. When the *News of the World* chortles 'Would you credit it? Curvy Caren's first job was as an insurance clerk', it vaguely assumes that insurance has something to do with credit. It hasn't. When the *Sunday Times* reports astonishingly that 'One third of black New Yorkers between the age of five and nineteen are murdered', it is probably misreading, as the *Spectator*'s excellent '...and statistics' spot pointed out, a statement that one third of deaths among black New Yorkers aged five to nineteen are homicides. Statistical errors are often the result of not reading copy carefully enough, or simply not grasping the principle of percentages in particular. If illiterals account for 10 per cent of a newspaper's text and they rise *by* 10 per cent, they have gone *up* 1 per cent (10 per cent of 10 per cent). Most papers would have ILLITERALS UP 10%, which would be scaremongering. A common Fleet Street fault.

Some random traps awaiting the unwary, or the untutored:

Different from, not different to.

DEPRESSED MAN HUNG HIMSELF is wrong. The sub-editor should have hanged himself

Less is not the same as *fewer*. Less volume, fewer units. The slogan on a full-page ad for the Employment Training scheme carried by most national papers, A MILLION LESS SCHOOL LEAVERS WON'T MEAN A MILLION LESS JOBS, should have had less exposure or fewer errors.

To *effect* is to accomplish, to *affect*, to influence.

To *imply* is to suggest, to *infer*, to deduce.

Verbal does not really mean the same as oral, although it has been said that verbal sex means talking about it. All agreements are verbal. Unwritten agreements are oral.

Theatres put on *revues,* not reviews.

There is no such word as *miniscule.*

It is not *all right* to make alright one word.

You would think that everyone knew the *hopefully* pitfall by now. It is to be hoped that everyone will, one day.

Imaginary rules

Along with their visible style book, most newspapers seem to maintain an invisible, unwritten style book full of imaginary rules for the harassment of the journalist who cares about English. Some of the commonest:

1. An intro must consist of a specific number of lines according to its position in the paper. This particularly applies to regular features, where the paragraphing, at whatever cost to the style or sense of the piece, is made to follow the page scheme instead of the page scheme following the paragraphing.

2. A new leg cannot commence with a new paragraph. This leads to running on of paragraphs with the absurd results discussed in PARAGRAPHS.

3. Certain words, such as *university* and *government*, must be given a capital letter irrespective of whether their use is specific or general. The *Daily Mirror* once put a contributor to the absurdity of saying that the European Parliament was not a European Government – thus giving the accolade of a capital letter to an institution which does not exist.

4. The subject of a sentence must be seen to be believed. Not so. This is what a journalist wrote:

> I have been spending the last few days in the United States. Saw a couple of shows and solved the President's energy problem.

This is what appeared in print:

> I have been spending the last few days in the United States, saw a couple of shows and solved the President's energy problem.

The 'correction' – apparently made in the belief that the second sentence lacks a subject (it doesn't: the subject *I* is implied) – robs the passage not only of its style but of its grammar. The fused 'sentence', in the form presented, is governed by the auxiliary verb *have*, and one cannot say *I have saw a couple of shows*.

5. *Only* must be placed as near as possible to the word it qualifies. This arises from a common pedantic fear that *only* in the sense of *no more than* (*I have* only *one pen*) may be mistaken for *only* meaning alone (*I* only *have one pen*), or that *only* meaning *as*

recently as (*I bought it* only *today*) might similarly be confused (*I* only *bought it today*). In fact the serious possibility of confusion in the reader's mind does not arise very often, and in any case, *no more than* and *only* can mean substantially the same thing. *Drink to me* only *with thine eyes* does not differ materially from *Drink* only *to me with thine eyes*. It just scans better.

6. Infinitives cannot be split. They can, where fusing them makes for clumsiness. The needless repair of split infinitives when they were split on purpose, and are all the better for it, is infuriating enough to the journalist with an ear for English; it is even more maddening when the infinitive was not split (i.e. the separation of *to* from its verb by an adverb, as in *to really meddle*) in the first place. Anyone who thinks that *to be really meddled with* or *to have just meddled* is an example of a split infinitive, should not meddle.

As guidelines, imaginary rules may serve a purpose. Followed slavishly, they serve only the pedant.

Whether self-imposed or not, rules were made to be broken.

NOTE: The above dispensation does not apply to anything laid down in this manual. This is the rule that proves the exception.

The incredible blob

Fowler's *Modern English Usage*, second edition, revised by Sir Ernest Gowers (1965), expresses no views on the usage of blobs. It is therefore up to this manual to lay down first principles.

Blobs in our newspapers have what city planners would call a multi-purpose use. There are sometimes so many of them that the papers resemble Cook's International Railway Timetable.

One edition of the *Sun* had a blob content of over fifty, strewn indiscriminately about the paper to mark the beginnings of boxed paragraphs, to brighten up picture captions, to punch home a couple of points in a story, to highlight Ten Things You Didn't Know about an oil sultan, and so on. That they were distributed haphazardly was evidenced by the following day's *Sun*, where the blob count was down to eight. *The Times*, on the other hand, had twenty-two. It is not only the tabloids which are addicted.

Blobs should not be inserted into a page of type like plums in a pudding. It is not their function simply to jolly up the text. Nor should they be called upon to celebrate the extraordinary coincidence that three sentences in a row happen to begin with the word *He*. Blobs have specific uses, the main ones being:

- To itemize a genuine list or catalogue.

(For bogus lists and catalogues, see LISTS.)

- To mark a footnote.
- To mark an addendum to a story, such as, say, a comment from the City editor on a parliamentary finance report.
- To itemize a series of examples or anecdotes – the purpose here being to make it clear to the reader when the text is returning to its general drift.
- To refer the reader to another item in the paper.

In short, the blob is an aid to clarity or a means of claiming attention, not simply a cosmetic aid. If it is doing no more for the page than could be done by a squashed fly, leave it out.

Inelegant variation

'Two pints of stuff, a stuff and tonic and a packet of stuff'

Most books about the use of words warn writers against *elegant variation* – e.g. 'the penultimate month of the year' as another way of saying November.

In the uncouth world of Fleet Street, where space is tighter than in the three-volume Victorian novels from which the textbooks seem to draw most of their examples of living English, elegant variation is not much of a problem. But *inelegant variation* is.

> Sugar rots your teeth and probably shortens your life. Britain annually devours 2½ tons of the stuff .

Thus a *Daily Express* writer who could just

conceivably be using *the stuff* in its pejorative sense, as in *stuff and nonsense*, but who, if numerous other examples of *the stuff* are any guide, is far more likely to be stuck for a synonym. But why should he want one? By putting a full stop after *tons* he could have saved himself the trouble. By recasting those two sentences altogether, he could have taken on more trouble but avoided the problem.

The stuff is not the most clodhopping of journalism's inelegant variations but it is one of the most common. It is our contribution to the commodities market. There is no raw material, from cocoa to zinc, that has not been described as *the stuff* in print. A broker who kept a tally of the number of times *the stuff* has been used for porridge or treacle or tobacco could set up a flourishing futures market in this flaccid general synonym.

But we can do worse than that:

> Cheers! Britain is on a beer bender. Last year we drank a staggering 2,000m gallons of mild, bitter and keg – a foaming 40 pints for every pub-crawler.
>
> That's nearly seeing double on the hangover figures of five years ago. And elbow-lifting is still on the increase…

The story is made up, but the style is not. It is possible to go on in that strain for another nine or ten inches without repeating the key word *beer*.

Fleet Street has more synonyms for drinking and eating than Roget ever dreamed of. In newspaper stories we are permitted to eat and drink only in the first paragraph. Thereafter we guzzle. We knock back. We put away. We lower. We lap up. We nosh. We chomp. We slurp. We chew our way through. We sink our teeth into. We get on the outside of. We down. We swig.

As often as not, *the stuff* features in these contortions.

Inelegant variation is not by any means confined to food and drink but these examples will suffice. The mannerism is easily cured. Before conjuring another of these contrived synonyms out of the air, ask what is wrong with repeating the original word. If it sounds stilted, try a pronoun (*it* is surprisingly under-used for so short a word). If it still doesn't seem right, try re-phrasing so that the second or third repetition isn't necessary. If this means cutting out a sentence or two, it is probably all to the good: much inelegant variation comes about from spinning a story out beyond its worth.

A variation on inelegant variation, courtesy of the *Daily Mirror*:

> Prince Andrew coughed up £10,000 for the pair of lead-covered towers...

Coughed up avoids saying the Prince *paid* £10,000. But this was no avoidance of repetition. The writer, for mysterious reasons of his own, simply wanted to avoid using the everyday straightforward verb.

The intro

There are basically only three kinds of newspaper intro – the one that starts to tell a news story, the one that starts to sell a news story, and the one that starts to tell a story.

To dispose of the middle one first:

> Stop gnashing your teeth at men, girls – and start feeling some sympathy for the poor mixed-up things.

That sells the story, which then commences:

Former GP Dr Vernon Coleman yesterday claimed that men are an oppressed minority in terms of sex, pensions, health, divorce and jobs.

That tells the story. The first paragraph, of course, is completely superfluous. This breezy approach is best left to features and in any case should be used sparingly. Nor must the breeziness descend into outright banality.

Turning to the other two types of intro, which account for the mass of news stories, the difference is between *Detectives were last night hunting the mastermind behind the kidnapping of an Arab millionaire*, and *It was 3.41 on Friday when a slightly-built, quietly-spoken Kuwaiti businessman finished his coffee in the Peacock Room of the International Hotel...*

The latter technique was closely identified with the *Sunday Times*. In fact it was pioneered by the *Sunday Express*, which for years featured stories where the whole point seemed to be that it was a perfect day for two old friends to enjoy a game of golf. It was only in paragraph five that they found the body.

The tabloid version of the narrative style is found under CONSEQUENCES. On its classic *Sunday Times* form, only two points need to be made. The first is that the story had better be good. The reporter, or more likely reporting team, needs a far more detailed picture than the colleague phoning *Detectives were last night hunting* from notes on the back of a cigarette packet. The story opened in this way must have, to support its leisurely beginning, a gripping middle and an intriguing end (even though the end may be nowhere near the conclusion of what could well be a running story).

Secondly, because the narrative intro keeps the reader waiting, it has to grab him, though not necessarily by the lapel. In its *Sunday Express* form, the model seems to be Somerset Maugham. The *Sunday Times* model may owe something to the James Bond novels. Not surprisingly – Ian Fleming was a *Sunday Times* man.

The straight intro produces few problems but many pitfalls. All it has to do is to meet the objection raised by the editor in the Hecht-MacArthur play 'The Front Page': 'Who the hell ever reads the second paragraph?' The first paragraph has to contain the essence of the story in perhaps twenty-five words.

The secret is in deciding which is the story. Here is an intro that can't make up its mind:

> Planners are backing a proposed £30,000 greyhound training track after opponents were branded snobs.

The reporter is trying to weave the story's two strands into one to give them equal importance by making it appear that one element is a consequence of the other. The uneasy and unstylish juxtaposition of *are backing* and *were branded* shows that he is in trouble. The truth is that however the facts are arranged, one half of the story is going to dominate the other. The intro must therefore read something like this:

> Opponents of the proposed £30,000 greyhound training track heard themselves branded as

'snobs' at last night's planning meeting.

But despite their objections the planners backed the scheme.

Or like this:

Planners are backing a proposed £30,000 greyhound training track despite objections from residents.

Opponents heard themselves branded as 'snobs' at last night's planning meeting.

Either will work. What Hecht and MacArthur really should have said was: 'Who the hell ever reads the second paragraph if the first paragraph doesn't grab their attention."

I say, I say

With a little patience, a mynah bird might be taught to recite these exclamatory opening words to various news stories and features:

'Allo, 'allo
Begorrah!
Blimey!
Brr!
Brr-brr, brr-brr!
Calling all disco fans!
Calling all kids!
Calling all stamp collectors!
Cheers!
Cor! Strike a light!
'Ello 'ello 'ello!

G'day, possums!
Help!
I say, I say!
Mornin', mornin'!
Oh, baby!
Oh, boy!
Oh, brother!
Ouch!
Phew!
Vroom vroom!
Wakey wakey!
Whacko!
What a smasher!
What a turn-up!
Whoops!

Leave exclamations to exclamation marks. An interesting story does not have to open with a war-whoop.

See also WHAT ROT.

Italic and bold

Fowler is as reticent on bold type as he is on blobs. But he is positively garrulous on *italics*, the third of this trio of cosmetic failsafes.

'Printing a passage in italics,' begins Fowler acidly, 'is a primitive way of soliciting attention.' Had his newsagent delivered the *Sun* instead of *The Times Lit. Supp.?*

Tabloid typography solicits so much attention with its italics that when it comes to their legitimate use – to stress a word, for example – it has to resort to bold type. But since it uses bold italics also as 'a primitive way of soliciting attention', they are often not enough either. It has to be underlined bold italics – then bold Roman – then bold Roman capitals.

This is typographical inflation.

The tabloids' use of italic and bold runs to no fixed pattern. On some pages, every third paragraph or so is set in a different face from the body-type. On others, even though there may be much longer stretches of text and therefore a greater excuse for breaking the page up, italic and bold are not used at all. But that is the exception, not the rule – an exception made up for by entire features elsewhere in the paper being set in bold *and* bold italic.

A computer programmed to random-select passages for setting in a different typeface could do the job as efficiently as any sub-editor. The rule seems to be: where a story has been going on for four inches or more, set the next bit in italic or bold or both, in case the sheer monotony of ploughing through 120 words at a stretch should cause the reader's mind to wander. Logically, of course, there is no reason why these variants should stop at italic and bold: were the tabloids less conservative, the odd paragraph could be set in Gothic or Billboard.

The trouble with shrieking type is that if a newspaper goes on bellowing at the top of its voice, it is going to be hard put to claim its readers' particular attention when it really has got something to shout about. The *Sun*, in what its subs would probably call a bold move, has attempted to resolve this boy crying wolf situation by setting key words in the body of the story in bold capitals. Thus, in the course of a page or two, one may read that superstar Elton John was **STUNNED** by an attack on a journalist by his staff, and has given his manager a **ROCKET;** that football fans acquitted of hooliganism **CUDDLED** girl jurors and **SCREAMED** 'Sieg Heil' after the court had heard that police may have **ADDED** notes to their logs to strengthen their case; that a **BURGLAR** has been made a store **DETECTIVE** with the job of **STOPPING** other thieves at a big store **DESPITE** his past record; and that a DIY hubby who blew his top and used a **BUZZ SAW** to hack up his home **CARVED UP** the three-piece suite and **TORE** into a nest of tables, then minutes later was **CUTTING** lumps out of the telly and **CHOPPING** chunks from curtains, carpets and cushions.

Since one edition of the *Sun* had over eighty words emphasized in this way, quite apart from the usual quota of random passages set in bold and underlined italic, it is to be feared that the paper may be in for an attack of collective laryngitis.

To return to ordinary italics, their proper uses are too well known to need summarizing. In any case, they are to found in Fowler, who concludes his italics article on this sour note: 'To italicize whole sentences or large parts of them as a guarantee that some proportion of what one has written is really worth attending to is a miserable confession that the rest is negligible.'

Bold type, however, should be used for just the purpose that Fowler castigates: to draw the reader's attention to the really important or dramatic passages in a longish story.

Italic and bold can be used to good effect as an integral part of the story's presentation. An excellent example is to be found under WHAT IS STYLE?

Individual words should not be set in bold for the sake of stressing them. This job should be given back to italic. However, the *Sun*'s technique of highlighting fairly interesting words in bold would be better abandoned altogether than relegated to italic.

Italics should *never* be let loose on a joke. If the joke is funny, italics will kill it. If it is not funny, italics will simply embarrass it.

Jargon

Journalists who would not dream of using the jargon of their own trade in a report, say, of a newspaper takeover bid will cheerfully use the jargon of other fields that come into the news.

It is jargonese, not journalese, that impels the *Observer* to record, 'Journalism input comes almost entirely from agency reports.'

This is the kind of journalism input that is appearing daily in American papers: 'PanAm reported no upturn in traffic flow yesterday. "There's been no onrush," a PanAm spokeswoman said.' [PanAm, the airline, collapsed in 1991]

Strunk and White complain, in their admirable *The Elements of Style,* 'Why must jails, hospitals, schools suddenly become "facilities"?' Because when the authorities decided as a cosmetic exercise that jails would be *correctional facilities,* the newspapers tamely followed suit, that's why.

Expressions such as *in-house, on-air transmission, in-car entertainment, hospitalization, transportation, game plan,* have all sidled into the ever-hospitable columns of our newspapers from other people's jargon. But to use outsiders' jargon is to take their own evaluation of themselves on trust – or anyway, to give the impression of doing so. That is one good reason why specialists should never resort to the jargon of the field they cover. The other good reason is that it baffles the reader.

Never assume that you are writing only for the initiated. A distinguished economics writer in *The Times*, diffidently approached by a sub who could not make head or tail of one of his columns, is supposed to have said, 'That piece is meant to be understood by only a dozen people, and you're not one of them.' If the story is not apocryphal, he was a better economist than a journalist.

Do not borrow computer terms – *user friendly, download, bug, inbox, spam, hardware, reboot.* They will worm their way into the language soon enough without your help.

Never use sets of initials, except those in everyday use such as TUC, EU, without first spelling them out – *International Monetary Fund (IMF)*. If necessary (that is, if you had to look it up), go on to spell out what the title or term means – *guardian of the free world's money system*. Sometimes the words sheltering behind the initials are as impenetrable as the initials themselves.

Paraphrase rather than use jargon in a quote.

"All children upon attaining the age of five years must be paid for at the appropriate rate," a Transport Department spokesman confirmed.

He may well have done, but all he meant was that children over five must be paid for.

Helping the police with their inquiries and *gained access to the rear of the premises* is desk sergeant talk, not news desk talk. *He could neither confirm nor deny that an inquiry had been ordered into the incident* should in the first place read *He* would *neither confirm, etc.;* but far better would be *He would not say if an inquiry had been ordered. Attacker,* not *assailant.*

Use of *conference* and *management* without the definite article is for politicians and trade unionists, not journalists.

Public bodies and business corporations have a vested interest in persuading everyone to speak their unspeakable Dalek language. It is a brainwashing operation against which the press should be fiercely resistant.

PS: But are the Daleks as appalled by our jargon – *slam, swoop, mercy dash,* etc. – as we are by theirs?

Journalese

Clampdown!

Tabloidese, with its *raps*, *bids*, *probes* and so forth, is discussed elsewhere. *Journalese* is what is indulged in by non-tabloid journals. It can be almost as jarring.

In an unprecedented move signalling a ferocious new crackdown... The urgent prose conjures up a dashing image of an intrepid foreign correspondent phoning down a crackly line from the only hotel bar left standing in some far-off trouble spot. *A gold dealer who fleeced his clients to finance a lavish lifestyle of champagne and fast cars...* Here one visualizes the stereotype reporter in the belted raincoat, frantically tapping away against a deadline on a battered Remington between mouthfuls of cheese sandwich.

Reporting, unless it is of the personalized James Cameron or John Pilger variety, should not summon up even a vague picture of the reporter. The words should not intrude on the message they are conveying. The reason they do so is that they are selected for their pushiness. No one else writes like this: journalese is an exercise in stringing together words and phrases used nowhere else but in journalism:

> Mrs Thatcher is *backing* Prince Charles in his *bid* to *curb* sex and violence on television, it was *revealed* last night.
>
> She has *given the go-ahead* for a *battery* of *new controls* to ensure programmes are fit for family viewing when a broadcasting *free-for-all* is *unveiled* next month.
>
> The *curbs* will be far more stringent than TV *chiefs* expected, and the Government is *braced* for protests that they are being *shackled* and censored…

In journalese, *shock reports* forever *call* on the government, which in turn is *set* to make *sweeping changes*. Plans are *under attack* or *facing broadsides*, commitments are *spelled out*, remarks are *certain to spark off a new political storm*, steps are *urged to curb growing menaces*, ministers *sound clear warnings*, new developments *pose a threat*, new crises *loom*, new crazes *reach epidemic proportions*… There are so many *dramas* in the dramatic world of journalese that when one reads an *Independent* headline CHANNEL 4 EXPANDS DRAMA, one reads on in expectation of a drama involving Channel 4's territorial ambitions rather than an account of how Channel 4 proposes to expand its drama output.

Like tabloidese, journalese is not the most reliable conveyor of the English language:

> Margaret Thatcher is actively contemplating a fundamental restructuring of Whitehall departments which could lead to a crucial new political role for Cecil Parkinson...

Thus, breathlessly, the *Sunday Times,* incidentally dressing its journalistic mutton as lamb by the use of expensive words like *contemplating* and *fundamental restructuring* rather than *re-thinking* and *radical change.* But the *Sunday Times* could not resist *crucial* from the lexicon of journalese. Crucial, however, does not mean important in the straightforward sense, but essential to the resolving of a crisis, significant. The word has been selected for its souped-up quality of being more dramatic than the proper one. If *important* wasn't important enough for the story, then the selection of *key* from the journalese vocabulary would at least have had the merit of being less misleading.

Journalese, expertly and sparingly used, helps give a newspaper its flavour, its character of being a newspaper rather than a copy of *Hansard* or a court transcript. In large doses it can be clammy and claustrophobic as the reader struggles to extricate himself from a morass of *moves, clampdowns, crackdowns, pledges, clashes* and *stalemates.*

No story ever lost impact by being told in plain English.

Just-so stories

The conclusions reached later in these pages about *really* (see OH, REALLY?) apply just as much to *just:*

> Just why are the Government taking mortgages out of the cost-of-living index?

Why *just why*? Why not just *why*?

The same question may be asked about *just who, just how, just what, just when, just where, just one of those things, just good friends, just the job* and *just purrfect*, all of which regularly take up much-needed space in newspaper columns.

Kneejerks

Ladies' underwear, lavatories and private parts have a chortling fascination for schoolboys, end-of-pier comedians – and popular newspapers.

Show a tabloid sub a story about someone being locked in a lavatory and he will show you a headline containing the word FLUSHED and a re-write containing the word *inconvenienced*.

Show him a story on the relative sizes of English and European backsides and he may dither between CHEEKY and BOTTOM LINE or BOTTOMS UP in his headline, but you may be sure that *gave the findings a bum's rush* will figure in the text.

Show him a story about an underwear firm laying off 800 workers and in a trice he will produce the headline BOTTOM FALLS OUT OF KNICKERS! and an intro to the effect that the knickers market is *in a twist*; while with his left hand dealing with a snippet about an underwear thief who left money for the garments he stole:

> NICKERS FOR YOUR KNICKERS
> A knicker-nicker left a few nicker for the woman he loved when he stole her underwear. For clipped to the washing line where her knickers had been was a £10 note…

This standard, self-parodying, sniggering approach is not so much the product of a schoolboy smutty mind as of a sub-editorial silted-up mind, where stories falling into a particular class attract a kneejerk reaction.

With a little coaching, anyone who has ever pulled a Christmas cracker could copy-edit at this level.

What does the victim of a 'flush prank' in a train loo do? He goes loco and sets off a chain reaction.

What kind of life does a mean, rich cat-lover lead her maid? A dog's life.

What did a tipsy top surgeon do when performing a cosmetic breast operation? Made a boob.

What did a 'bungling burglar' have when he injured himself on glass while breaking into a police office? A pain in the nick.

Kneejerk journalism is lazy journalism, reaching for the nearest joke – usually a Fleet Street chestnut. The philosophy of its practitioners, unspoken or otherwise, is that if this is what 'the punters' want, this is what they will get. What they mean is that since this is what 'the punters' will get, this is what they will want.

It needn't be so. The routine, kneejerk response to the story of a bride whose wedding dress ended up in a rubbish tip is that she was *really down in the dumps.* The *Daily Mirror* thought about it a fraction longer and came up with the non-kneejerk. *A bride felt like giving her dad away when he threw out her wedding gown with the rubbish.*

Lists

Dr Johnson used to walk along Fleet Street touching lamp posts. This mild case of obsessional mania seems to have been transmitted from generation to generation, for Fleet Street's present-day wordsmiths are victims of a very similar neurosis.

They have a compulsion towards *lists.* They cannot stop themselves arranging pieces of copy to resemble mail-order catalogues or railway timetables. They do it on the slightest excuse, leaping on any combination of words that, with the introduction of bold capitals, blobs (see THE INCREDIBLE BLOB) or other typographical gimmickry, can be passed off as tabulation:

       A student with sex problems turned his

dormitory room into a makeshift operating theatre.

He **PLACED** mirrors around the room to get a good view of his work;

DRAPED sterilized sheets over the furniture.

WORE a surgeon's mask and gloves and

SWALLOWED barbiturates as an anaesthetic.

This means the teachers will

REFUSE to supervise children at lunch breaks

REFUSE to take part in outside activities

REFUSE to use their own cars on school business

Later Mr Orion, a foreman at the building site, told colleagues about the night visit.

Then the blacking really started.

THE foreman's association decided not to work with Mr Clapp.

MOST of the 350 men on the site are being laid off.

AND Mr Clapp has taken a week's holiday.

The entries against the girls' names included disclosures such as:

- 'Mother ran off.'
- 'Adoption in the family.'
- 'Being treated for psychological problems.'

In the first of these extracts, four parts of the same sentence have been arranged in a list apparently because they all begin with verbs; in the second, a list has been manufactured by the unnecessary repetition of REFUSE; in the third, it is anybody's guess why the words THE, MOST and AND have been picked out in capitals; and in the fourth, the principle has been followed that where three examples appear in a news story, each example must be preceded by a blob.

Except for the THE-MOST-AND combination, which defies analysis, the extracts quoted above can at least claim some vague affinity with the catalogue principle. There are examples without number of pronouns such as *he, it, they* being picked out in black and awarded a blob for no other reason than that they occur twice in successive sentences. Nor is it uncommon to find a sequence of paragraphs given the bold-and-blob treatment when not by any stretch of the imagination could it be called a list or catalogue. (Specialist articles are especially vulnerable to this treatment, it being a tenet of popular newspaper faith that anything written by specialists needs jollying up.)

A side product of the *list* obsession is the *in-and-out* syndrome:

> Gardening was too much of a slog for pensioner Daniel Keen. So was looking after a big cage of pet birds.
>
> The retired coalman decided to turn over a new leaf – by converting his garden into a plastic paradise.
>
> OUT went his 150 geraniums.
> OUT went his 50 budgerigars.
> IN came plastic flowers.
> IN came plastic budgies.
> IN came plastic toys and ornaments...

An index of popular newspaper stories where IN has come this and OUT has gone the other would make an impressive list in itself.

Typographical signposts indicating a list or catalogue should be used only when the list or catalogue is a genuine one – e.g. the recommendations of a report, the main points of a speech, the contents of a human ostrich's stomach as revealed by an X-ray.

Whether preceded by a blob, asterisk, star, number or any other symbol, the items in a list are still governed by its overall grammatical structure. It should be possible to attach each item in turn to the introductory matter and make a proper sentence.

Sentences should not be sub-editorially inverted, rearranged or given labels (BOOST No. 1, etc) to force them into a list sequence.

It is legitimate, and always tempting, to put a chapter of accidents in list form, but it can create difficulties, as in this example (where all the stops except the last one, incidentally, should be commas):

> During his eight-week jaunt Malcolm was:
> INVOLVED in a 100 mph road smash.
> HELD by a weird religious sect.
> ROBBED of his cash.
> BEATEN UP by villains and…
> JAILED for carrying a penknife.

The difficulty here is that so much compression has been necessary to get the events into list form that the entire story has to be gone over again:

In British Columbia a car in which he was travelling hit a ditch at 100 mph.

In San Francisco he was held a virtual prisoner by a religious sect...

And so on. THE INVOLVED-HELD-ROBBED list in effect robs the news pages of nine lines.

Little by little

So many little folk are to be found in the tabloids that they sometimes seem to be aimed at leprechauns.

It is true that there are fewer *little old ladies* inhabiting the news columns than there used to be, but there is still a wide choice of little people. The thinking seems to be that in any story about a child, the reader will prefer a vague size category first and the age later:

> Little love child Zita Icke won £21,000 damages in the High Court yesterday... (Age of little love child: five – given in fifth paragraph.)

> When it comes to fighting big, big battles, Little Thumbelina is head and shoulders above the rest... (Age of Little Thumbelina: 15 weeks – given in second paragraph. Real name given in fourth paragraph.)

> Little Master Miracle goes home from hospital today... (Age of Little Master Miracle: 3 months – given in second paragraph. Real name given in third paragraph.)

> Little Emma Williams may not be old enough to drink, but she can go one better than the regulars in her dad's pub... (Age of little Emma: newly-born – we learn when she called 'Time' in the third paragraph.)

Children to whom the size code for some reason doesn't apply (perhaps they are big for their age?) are often described as *toddlers* or *tots*:

Toddler Kevin Carter pulled on his favourite red wellies, went out to play in the garden... and vanished.

How old is this toddler? See third paragraph. He is two.

In hard news rather than human-interest stories, these cuddly-toy euphemisms are never used at all:

> A boy aged nine was found brutally murdered last night...

In any story about children, the reader wants to know at once *How old?* Is it only in hard news stories that this natural appetite for hard facts can be satisfied in the first few words?

Metaphor and simile

To begin with what distinguishes one from the other: *over the moon* is a metaphor, *sick as a parrot* is a simile.

It is usual for English manuals to warn against the use of tired metaphors: *took the wind out of his sails, left him with egg on his face, wheel has come full circle,* etc., etc.

This manual would warn even against metaphors which have yet to reach their best sell-by date. A metaphor once coined is a used phrase. If literary convention required one to attribute its authorship, as it does with quotations that have not yet sunk into platitude, then *The wheel has come full circle, as Shakespeare's King Lear said* would be a reminder that one is stealing another man's clothes, however ragged. (Unfortunately *stealing another man's clothes* cannot be found in the *Oxford Dictionary of Quotations*.)

But, of course, literature accounts for only a fraction of our repertoire of metaphor. Hundreds of new metaphors rain on us daily, to be picked out of the (metaphorical) gutter by those who cannot be bothered to think of their own. The *Economist* style book quotes a clutch from its own field: *stem the deluge, wage explosion, put on ice, booms and busts, nest eggs, question mark over inflation,* etc. Every walk of life is similarly barnacled. (This last sentence is an example of *mixed metaphor*, which is to be avoided. A walk cannot be barnacled, even metaphorically.)

The JARGON of every trade or calling is gradually borrowed by others, to add to their stock of metaphor. So are other stray expressions that take the general fancy. Thus, during a single shift in Fleet Street, one may find oneself cooling one's heels, being given a bum steer, running around in circles, getting nowhere fast, flogging a dead horse, going into a flat spin, having kittens, being read the Riot Act, being shown the red card, falling off the wagon, drowning one's sorrows, feeling no pain, becoming legless, and going back to square one. It would need a Partridge to pin down the origins of all these phrases. But that is how language is born – and how it dies. A dead metaphor is like a skin shed by a snake.

None of this is to say that we should avoid using

metaphor. Indeed we cannot do without it. Omitting the quoted examples, this section has so far indulged itself in *best sell-by date, stealing another man's clothes, rain, picked out of the gutter, walk of life, barnacled,* and it is by no means over-larded – a metaphor taken from Mrs Beeton – with metaphor. (The dead snake is simile.)

There is even a case for worn metaphor, as there is a case for a comfortable pair of old slippers. Everyone knows what a chicken-and-egg situation is. The reader doesn't have to do any work. He knows what the expression means and he doesn't require an alternative. Why rack one's brains for a substitute – a God-and-universe situation, for instance? No – it doesn't work. You have to be aware of the original question: Which came first, God or the universe? before boiling it down into metaphor. So chicken-and-egg will take some shifting.

Yet by and large, to use a hackneyed phrase, the more hackneyed the phrase that first comes to mind, the more advisable it is to try for something new. To a journalist (as to anyone who cares about language), yesterday's metaphor should be like yesterday's news – already stale. *As fresh as new-mown hay* is as fresh as old paint.

The best colour writers, as they are somewhat patronizingly called by their hard-news colleagues, mint good metaphors, or spin an original twist on old ones. 'Police *ran a zip-fastener round* the village' makes a change from *'sealed off* the village', although the image is perhaps a little overblown for a news story. *Wolf in wolf's clothing, chickens come home to roast* and *scraping the bottom of the bran-tub* are nice variations on old themes. But – they have already been used. Back to that old metaphorical drawing-board.

Moving briefly on to *simile*, the same cautions and exhortations apply. Feature writers in particular get through a lot of similes – perhaps too many. Everything doesn't have to be like something else unless one wants to sound like a poor imitation of Raymond Chandler or a good imitation of Clive James.

Anyway, both metaphor and simile should always give way to a really striking phrase. 'Nobody in the whole house spoke enough Welsh to buy a stamp' (John Edwards, *Daily Mail*) is far more arresting than, say, 'They spoke as much Welsh as a family of Ghanaians.'

Whether in metaphor, simile or any other form, *literally* should be boycotted. If a man *literally died laughing* it would be front page news. But *literally* would be superfluous. Everything that happens, happens literally. If it doesn't, then it literally didn't happen.

More haste

The standard Fleet Street excuse for shoddy or silly writing has always been that the offending story has been written against the clock.

It usually isn't so.

Deadline fever encourages taut, crisp writing with a maximum of facts and a minimum of frills. The straightforward hard-news story, phoned virtually straight on to page one, rarely displays any of the faults discussed in this book.

The truly awfully written story, of the kind that ought to be hung on the walls of schools of journalism as an example of how not to do it, demands time.

The puns have to be sweated over, the laborious intro has to be re-worked again and again until it cannot possibly be any more forced, the jocular references have to be carefully strung together like blunt razor blades dangling from a magnet.

For a story about, say, an old lady who was flushed with embarrassment as a result of being locked in a town hall lavatory, and the consequent chain reaction when the council tried to get to the bottom of it, at least four hours should be allowed.

For a late-night train crash killing 100 people, allow twenty minutes.

Not only but also

Not only are the following two paragraphs not paragraphs, but one of them isn't even a sentence.

> Not only was this post box fixed with its slot nine feet above ground.
>
> For three weeks people put letters in it.

This follows the rule that says: if a sentence is long and dull, chop it in half and throw away the intervening conjunction. If the passage is still too long, make it into two paragraphs.

There is a codicil to the rule, which goes, 'And put in a crosshead.'

The best available example of how the split sentence/paragraph/crosshead technique can be used to baffle the reader:

Not only is some of the compensation offered inadequate.

CHARGED

Before you can find out whether you have been wrongly charged, you have to make sense of your bills.

Before you can find out what that crosshead is doing there, you have to make sense of the story.

The numbers game

Putting aside the doubtful ethics expressed therein, the following statement errs on the side of plurality:

> Gould's final warning: 'Vincent Jones has his destiny in his own hands. Every footballer must always err on the side of legality, no matter who they are.'

Wrong. No matter who *he is*.

The multi-million-dollar-saga... will be shunted off into the sidings later this month after its ill-starred inaugural run of less than twenty episodes.

Wrong. *Fewer* than twenty episodes.

> Good on Lord Wallace for telling Lord Spene that his plans to keep working mums at home is the wrong approach to unemployment.

Wrong. His plans *are* the wrong approach.

> Here's two Cup Final fans who certainly don't mind revealing their favourite sides.

Wrong. Here *are* two Cup Final fans. And finally:

> He was one of those rare people who enjoyed his money, his talent as a musical conductor – and his fame.

Completely wrong – but if it were made numerically correct the sentence would be absurd: *He was one of those rare people who enjoyed their money, their talents as musical conductors, and their fame.*

Plurals and singulars cause much confusion, not least when one is mistaken for the other. The following notes may be useful (see also *is/are* under GRAMMAR).

Fewer can be counted, *less* cannot (*fewer* sugar lumps, *less* sugar). *Few* can be plural or singular: there *have been* few, there *has been a* few.

Collective nouns can be singular or plural. Go by the sense. *The press* is *free* is correct, because we are talking about one body. But *the press* are *debating their freedom*, since one body cannot debate.

Similarly with plural nouns with a singular meaning. *Politics* is *the art of the singular,* because one art is one thing. But *Their politics* are *the same* or *His politics* are *not my politics,* because here p shared or divided.

When the subject is plural but the o quantity, use a singular verb: *Fifty mistakes* is *a lot of mistakes.* Otherwise: The verb follows the number of the subject, as in *His plans* are *the wrong approach.*

Contrary to a grammatical old wives' tale, *none* can be either singular or plural, as can *number.* Fowler recommends treating *number* as singular when it has a definite article (The number *present* was *large*) and plural when it has an indefinite article (A *large* number were *present*).

To each his own singular: *each, everybody, everyone,* are singular pronouns requiring singular verbs. But *Everyone to his or her desk, please* is schoolma'am English. Duck out of this confrontation if possible, otherwise use singulars as plurals so long as they don't jar.

Where the numbering is correct, but it still sounds vaguely incorrect, as in *Most people's problem is trying to hang on to their money,* re-cast it. *The problem most people have is in trying to hang on to their money.*

Headlines and accompanying matter must agree numerically. If 'Marks & Spencer *have* banned all their staff from accepting gifts from business contacts', then M & S BAN ON 'BRIBES' FOR *ITS* STAFF is wrong. If the headline says ROLLS *GET* ROUGH RIDE then the story should not begin 'Aerospace giant Rolls Royce *has* skidded off the runway.' (Perhaps it shouldn't begin that way in any case. See METAPHOR AND SIMILE.)

Officialese

Considering its reputation for independence, Fleet Street can still be curiously subservient towards officialdom. All too often *an official* or *officials* are quoted as if their officialdom were in itself proof of an unimpeachable source.

Officialdom is allowed a wide range of duties. 'Twist at your peril. That's what straight-laced officials warned when the dance craze swept the nation in 1961', reported the *Daily Mirror*. Which officials? Medical officials? Dance officials? Council officials?

Even if they cannot be named, officials should be identified. A Ministry of Defence spokesman isn't an official, he's a press officer.

And that's official is a phrase beloved of newspapers – again so much with the implication that what's official must be true that the phrase might as well read *And that's that*.

At least, in this context, the 'official' source is usually identified sooner or later. The formula is used as a device for streamlining opening paragraphs. By crossing out – say – *according to a report of the Office of Population Censuses and Surveys* and substituting *and that's official*, the journalist removes nine dead words from his intro, which now reads *We're living in luxury - and that's official...* The boring attribution may be found towards the end of the story – provided the sub remembers to leave it in.

Nobody wants the first sentence of a story cluttered up with longwinded titles; but *and that's official* does raise the question, how official? It should be answered as soon as possible so that the reader may judge whether the story is worth reading.

One more reason for reservations about *and that's official*: this venerable phrase, which is not only fossilized itself but has a tendency to fossilise any piece of writing to which it attaches itself, has been in use for at least sixty-five years. And that's official.

Oh, really?

The purpose of *really* in amateur doggerel of the 'Father sat on a pin/It really was a shame' variety is to pad out a line that otherwise would not scan.

It is difficult to detect its purpose in professional journalism. Yet a purpose it must have, for why else would it regularly crop up in newspaper stories?

> Tippling Tug Wilson could *really* take a lot on board. When he pushed the boat out in the boozer, he drank 15 pints a night...

> Do-it-yourself fanatic Michael Taylor *really* did for himself yesterday...

> Karen, 20, from Middlesex, had spells as a clerk, typist and window-dresser before she plumped for modelling... and now her career is *really* taking off.

> Pint-sized John May *really* stirred it up yesterday... by stealing a milk float...

In each case, *really* could be replaced by such aimless expressions as *actually, quite, definitely, absolutely, well and truly*, or, for the Irish editions, *entirely*:

> Tippling Tug Wilson could take quite a lot on board...

> Do-it-yourself fanatic Michael Taylor well and truly did for himself...

Now Karen's career is definitely taking off…

Didn't pint-sized John May stir it up entirely now…

Nothing is gained, nothing is lost, by the substitution. Then is *really* really necessary at all?

Tippling Tug Wilson could take a lot on board…

Do-it-yourself fanatic Michael Taylor did for himself yesterday…

Now Karen's career is taking off…

Pint-sized John May stirred it up yesterday…

None of these excerpts now looks quite right. There is a certain flatness there. It becomes apparent that the purpose of *really* is to provide an artificial boost for material – or anyway, the presentation of material – that would otherwise probably not grab the reader.

If news stories were subject to inspection by the public analyst, he would describe *really* as 0.1 per cent additional colouring matter.

Ooh la la

As Britain is sucked inexorably into Europe the proposition that foreigners are either funny or lesser breeds without the law of libel remains an unshakeable act of faith with the tabloids.

For the *Daily Star*, a 'glamour girl' TV actress now living in France has *gone to the frogs*.

For the *Sun*, a bogus 'top German cop' is a *fake Kraut*.

For the *Daily Mirror*, shoplifters coming over from France are *French knickers*.

Also for the *Mirror*, (but presumably not for its Scottish sister paper the *Daily Record*), a *Jock joker* who lifts his kilt for a video *McNasty* gives a bride an *och-eyeful*.

For the *News of the World*, a wife with an Arab 'toyboy' is a *Mustaffa missus,* while our lasses on the Golden Mile will really *sheik* Arabs who have turned Blackpool into a holiday *Mecca.*

At best, Fleet Street chauvinism is harmless schoolboy stereotyping with an awful comic postcard inevitability about it. British tourists (always *Brits* in foreign stories) kick up an El of a fuss at the Hotel Costabomb, Indian waiters try to curry favour, Japs have a yen to see the Queen, Irish labourers get into a paddy, Welshmen looking for a leak break into locked loos, look you, sportsmen from Denmark are Great Danes, drunks from Stockholm are Smashed Swedes, and no story involving Australians would be complete without a sprinkling of fair dinkums. As for the filthy French, it took a major TV series, *'Allo 'Allo,* to dislodge *Ooh la la* from the affections of sub-editors handling any story from Paris.

It is an act of faith that all foreign prisons are filthier and more unspeakable than our own. The *Daily Mirror* had a front-page picture of an imprisoned *Brit* in his airy Spanish cell which, with its big barred window overlooking a garden and its feel of spaciousness, compared favourably with, say, Wormwood Scrubs. Inevitably, it was a *hell-hole Spanish jail.*

At worst, the tabloids' insularity strays towards racism, where expelled Cuban diplomats are *Cuban heels* or where, in its Arabs in Blackpool story, the *News of the World* carries this unlikely quote from a hotelier: 'Sometimes they want to slaughter a sheep in the hotel. I don't allow that, though.'

There is a faint suggestion of Wogs beginning at Calais in this *Daily Star* report:

> The arena where fascist dictator Benito Mussolini delivered his bloodcurdling speeches has been declared a 'no-go' area for superstar Prince.
>
> For crackpot Romans say his fantastic laser show will 'lower the tone' of their snooty Stadium of Marbles.
>
> Now a furious Prince has told the high-falutin' Eyeties what they can do with their marbles…

Clearly the *Sun* and the *Daily Star* are confident that they know their audiences, otherwise the *Star* would hardly venture to headline a report of a political adventuress's impression that the Libyan leader may be 'either a homosexual or a mummy's boy', 'MAD DOG' GADDAFI'S A RAVING POOFTER. (It is interesting that the quotation marks are over the less contentious of the two epithets.)

Nor would the *Sun* cry quite so cockily, over a summary of a Press Council finding in its favour, YOU *CAN* CALL A POOF A POOF! Presuming that the Press Council did not express itself in quite those words, the *Sun* is talking to its readers on what it believes, perhaps justifiably, to be their level.

The *Daily Mirror*, which is as distanced from this kind of stuff as the *Independent* is from some tabloids' own page three girls, used to boast of being written in good doorstep English. At its best it still is.

Talk of *Krauts, Eyeties, dagoes, poofters* and the like is not doorstep English, it is the English of the blue club comedian and the drunk at the bar telling one for the road. It has no place in responsible journalism – or even irresponsible journalism, come to that.

Paragraphs

Fowler wrote that the purpose of paragraphing is to give the reader a rest. Had he been more of a student of the popular press he might have added that it is not the purpose of paragraphing to give the reader a jolt. That, however, is often the result.

Here is the intro of a feature on a visit by Elton John to Leningrad, as it appeared in print:

> Russia is in the throes of a new revolution... thanks to rock superstar Elton John. Of course, the fans have heard the music before.

The two sentences seem contradictory. If the reader takes up Fowler's suggestion of a rest at the end of the paragraph, it can only be because he needs time to work out what these apparent *non sequitors* add up to.

The story continues in paragraphs two and three:

> Expensive cassettes recorded from black market albums or from crackling, distorted broadcasts by the BBC World Service circulate among young people. But until now they haven't had the chance of seeing the phenomenon of a live rock concert.

All becomes clear – but in retrospect. The first sentence of the first paragraph ('Russia is in the throes of a new revolution... thanks to rock superstar Elton John') was meant to stand on its own. Either because that intro was deemed too short (see IMAGINARY RULES) or it didn't fit in with the page scheme, what should have been the opening sentence of the second paragraph was hooked on to it.

Had the paragraphing not been tinkered with, it would have fulfilled Fowler's other requirement: 'The paragraph is essentially a unit of thought, not of length; it must be homogeneous in subject-matter and sequential in treatment.'

In newspapers, however, the paragraph is essentially a unit of length, not of thought. This kind of treatment (the example is from the *Evening Standard*, but it could be from almost any paper) is common:

> But, like London Regional Transport, British

Rail is fighting a losing battle against graffiti 'artists'. My nearest BR station was recently redecorated in tasteful shades of buff, blue, grey, red and black, covering decades of grime dating back to the Steam Age.

Target

Overnight, the footbridge had been smothered in scribble. The workmen came back and repainted it. The following day, the graffiti had reappeared…

It is clear what the paragraph arrangement should be here – paragraph one should be the proposition, paragraph two the example. The way it has turned out, the first chunk consists of paragraph one and half of paragraph two. There is then a crosshead, followed by the rest of paragraph two.

At least the sense is not lost. Here is another example (one of many) of the paragraph arrangement working against the text:

The Prince Regent, 'Prinny', was a crazy punter. He had a runner that started hot favourite for the Derby and came in last.

The horse ran again the next day – unfancied – and won at a big price. The jockey got into serious trouble and was warned off. But Prinny later gave him a pension – which makes you wonder. King William IV was more interested in ships, so when his trainer asked him which of three horses he wished to be entered in a race in Derby week, he replied: 'Send the whole fleet.'

Some readers might conclude that the Prince

Regent and William IV were one and the same, and wonder not only why he gave the jockey a pension but how ships got into the story.

Even non-historians in newspaper offices will guess that there is a disguised 'widow' in that baffling second paragraph. The story turned into a new leg on the second half of the word 'wonder' – which should have ended a paragraph. To avoid leaving the syllable '-der' hanging on a top line (see IMAGINARY RULES again – or better still, do some rejigging so that the problem doesn't occur), the stray syllable was hitched to the nearest paragraph.

To sum up: paragraphs should make the story easier to read, not harder.

And a final word from Fowler: 'There can be no general rule about the most suitable length for a paragraph; a succession of very short ones is as irritating as very long ones are wearisome.'

The pay-off

Daily Mirror mythology has it that years ago, when there was a craze for 'delayed drop' stories, the paper ran a human-interest yarn about an old lady who painted flowers. The report rambled on about her artistic merits and grasp of botanical detail for seven inches or so, and then abruptly petered out without explaining the paper's sudden and unusual interest in artistic matters. It turned out that the vital last line of the story, *For she is blind*, had been lopped off on the stone to make it fit the page.

There are not many stories which would suffer so disastrously from having their last lines removed. With many, it could only be an improvement.

Here we have the *Daily Mirror* again, with a story about a self-appointed censor who cuts offending passages out of library books to the annoyance of one Alec, 68, who says the cuts make nonsense of some of the stories:

Wait for the pay-off:

> And Alec is a retired shoemaker. He knows a load of old cobblers when he sees it.

The stone-sub could have done his paper a favour by emulating the library book censor.

An encore from the same paper, rounding off a story about a soccer idol who has made a record called 'Head Over Heels In Love', using top stars Smokie as a backing group.

Which, if you want to get to the top, must be
the right way up.

The pay-off, appended only because the story is a
victim of FACETIOUSNESS and seems to demand one,
is pure gibberish.

Newspaper stories, even supposedly funny ones,
are not jokes. They do not need punchlines.
Nowhere does straining for effect show up more
than in contrived pay-offs. Unless the line is a good
one, apposite to the story and not an editorial
comment, it is best left out.

Person to person

If the story involves the reader, then involve the reader. Use the second person, not the third person.

This makes a dull-sounding provincial competition sound even duller.

> Every reader who would like to take part should enter his or her car number…

Calling all motorists would almost have been better. What's wrong with *If you would like to take part…*?

Always avoid the pedantic *his or her*, especially if they are about to become *their* at any moment.

Polysyllables

Most newspaper style books contain a catalogue of long or ponderous words which they recommend should be replaced, where possible, by shorter ones – *approximately* (about), *manufacture* (make), *establish* (set up), *permit* (let), *participate* (take part) and so on.

This style book is in favour of not using long words when short words will do, provided the short words are not examples of TABLOIDESE (e.g. *probe* for *investigation*), and just as importantly, that the short words know what the long words are talking about. This is not always the case.

Utilize does not mean *use*, as some style books advise. It means *make use of*.

Nor (another common style book recommendation) is *following* quite the same as *after*. *Following their appearance at the Theatre Royal, the Five Fol-de-rols are disbanding* suggests a decision made consequent upon what sounds like a disastrous appearance. *After their appearance at the Theatre Royal,* etc. suggests what they had already made up their minds to do before the appearance.

Demonstrate is not necessarily the same as *show*. When you demonstrate an egg-whisk at the Ideal Home Exhibition, you do more than show it.

Currently does not quite mean *now*. Compare *The Five Fol-de-rols are currently touring* with *The Five Fol-de-rols are now touring*.

An *experiment* is not necessarily a *test*.

Superfluous is not the same as *surplus*.

Anticipate is not the same as *expect*.

Aggravate is not the same as *annoy*.

Enormity does not mean *size*.

Fortuitously does not mean *luckily*.

Gratuitously does not mean *freely*.

Long words often have a grander family tree than short ones, and so are capable of wider and more subtle shades of meaning. Check with the dictionary. If the short word blunts the meaning of the word it is aiming to replace, or it is just plain wrong, leave the long word be, however polysyllabic.

Possessions

A BBC news-reader was heard to announce that a detective had flown from Singapore's Raffles Hotel to London's Heathrow to continue inquiries in London's Mayfair.

The possessive gazetteer – *Birmingham's New Street, Liverpool's Mersey, Brighton's West Pier, Cornwall's St Ives,* etc. – is now in use everywhere, except in the everyday English used by newspaper readers.

Although it has no purpose and doesn't save space (*Birmingham's New Street* is in fact one en *longer* than *New Street, Birmingham*) it is harmless enough – as is a nervous tic.

Puns and wordplay

On 17 June 1952, the following thought from Lord Beaverbrook was conveyed to the staff of the *Daily Express* via their editorial bulletin:

> *Once Britten twice shy* is a pun that will amuse some people and irritate others. We should rigorously, vigorously ban puns in headlines and text.

It was one more Beaverbrook cause that was doomed to failure. Today it is not only the *Daily Express* but all national newspapers – and the provincial evening papers that emulate the national tabloids, and the bright web-offset weeklies that emulate the provincial evening papers – that cannot resist a good pun. Or, for that matter, a bad one.

What is remarkable about the following story?

BY GUM! THOSE BOOKIES
FACED A STICKY PROBLEM

One hundred London bookmakers faced a sticky situation when a quick-drying superglue was used to seal their front doors, it was disclosed yesterday.

Last night they were adhering to a theory that it could have been Scottish football fans on their way to Wembley who had gummed up the works last Saturday...

The remarkable thing is not that the story contains five puns in sixty-one words. That is about par for the course. The remarkable thing is that the story appeared in the *Daily Telegraph*. Time was when a *Telegraph* man turning in such stuff would have been given sick leave.

The *Telegraph* overlooked the point, made in the *Daily Mirror*, that the sticky campaign gave the bookies a right old pasting. But then the *Mirror* was the pathfinder in this field. At a time when other papers were injecting puns and *double entendres* only into the occasional headline, as complained of by Beaverbrook, the *Mirror*'s punsters were already making forays into the text. As long ago as June 1939, the *Mirror* was chortling:

The writing on the wall is plain – the Welsh language must either adapt itself to its modern environment or perish, says the Welsh Department...

Forty years on, the *Mirror* was still savouring the joke:

> The writing's on the wall for FBI fingerprint experts...

The paper that was forty years before its time (or forty years after its time, depending on how one looks at it) with the writing-on-the-wall gag can claim some other notable firsts.

It was the first paper to call women police officers *fair cops* (a joke still wheeled out once a year on what is probably its anniversary); the first to use the adjective *purrfect* in connection with cats; the first to use the headline TEACHERS CANED (now thoroughly refurbished and modernized as SIR CANED); the first to use the caption intro *Eye eye!* when what were then called pin-ups had a nautical theme; and the first, at the dawn of the permissive society, to describe two other pin-ups (by then known as page three girls) as *bosom pals*.

But all that was back in the heady pioneering days. How is the *Daily Mirror* placed in the punning race in a more sophisticated era when the new technology can inject up to twenty-five puns into a column of type without any human being having to use his hands or even his head? Alas, the *Daily Star* has long ago overtaken its rival, in simpers if not in circulation.

CYCLE-OGICAL WARFARE
Swiss roll out a silent army

By the left, quick PEDAL! Switzerland's mighty war machine rolls into battle… on bikes.

And why not? Hitler's crack troops had their Nuremberg Raleighs…

Now the crafty Swiss, who haven't fired a shot in anger since Hannibal crossed the Alps on an elephant, have gone cuckoo over the idea.

Their army is spending £4m on shiny new bikes for its boneshaker battalions.

Presumably, the top brass follow up behind… in Swiss Rolls!

Valiantly, the *Mirror* hit back with the headline WOULD YUGO HERE? on a report on a Yugoslav holiday resort overlooking a mineral process plant. The *Daily Express* pitched in with TV-AM EARLY BIRDS ARE A SNORE POINT, *The Times* with SCOT NATS BUZZ AGAIN, the *Independent* with GLASFROST on an item about the difficulties of getting a car repaired in Archangel, near the Arctic Circle, and the *Daily Telegraph* with SPARE PARTS THIEVES TOOK HOOVER TO THE CLEANERS. *Today* entered GALLOPING MAJOR CAN MAKE MINT FROM POLO, and the *Daily Mail* bravely rose to the challenge:

CROC BITES OFF THE
HAND THAT FED IT

You have to hand it to single-handed Alf Casey.

His crocodile Charlene bit off the one that fed

it, and though her 71-year-old master says he can no longer chance his arm taking her to the pub for a drink , there are no hard feelings…

He admits, however: 'When I give her a little scratch these days I keep her at arm's length.'

As for the *Guardian*, it managed within the space of a single sports section to offer its readers PROLIFIC THACKRAY MAKES WIDNES VANITY FAIR; LABOURED EXCHANGE; DAVIS WASHES OUT WHITE; ANOTHER JANGLING FOR SHAKY SPURS; and, in references to the Harlequins scrum-half Richard Moon, a West Ham player named Ward and Worcestershire's Gordon Lord respectively, MOON SHOT, EMERGENCY WARD and RESPECTFUL LORD'S DAY OBSERVANCE.

But when all was said and punned it was the *Sun* which took the laurels:

OH WATT A LOVER!
Electric groom gives his bride
a shock in bed

Human dynamo Richard Durbin makes the sparks fly when he cuddles his newlywed wife Lucinda.

But after a week of marriage she has kicked him out of bed – because she got ELECTRIC SHOCKS every time he gave her watt for.

Doctors say the volt farce is caused by a massive build-up of static electricity in Richard's body, and there is no way to switch it off.

Short-fused Lucinda, 22, said yesterday: 'Making love isn't supposed to feel like sitting in the electric chair... "

Live wire Richard, of Boston, Massachusetts, said: 'This has been with me ever since I started dating... '

Lucinda, who works with Richard in his insurance business, is threatening to throw him out of house and ohm if he can't find a solution...

Inviting its readers to share the joke, or rather to prolong it, the *Sun* then adds a footnote: 'SOCKET TO US. Is your partner an ohm-loving bright spark? Tell us your funny stories about static electricity and win a pair of bedtime wellies.'

Truly the Fleet Street pun has travelled far – and with any luck may travel farther.

Such examples, plucked from scores readily to hand, may convey the flavour of puns and wordplay as they appear in popular (and not so popular) newspapers, but it is difficult to convey their cumulative effect. What has to be remembered is that these are not stray puns or isolated puns or occasional puns, but that they appear *every* day on practically *every* page of *every* tabloid. On the particular day that this paragraph was being written, for example, readers of the *Sun* and the *Daily Star* (the *Mirror* was for once relatively pun-free) were able to learn that page three stunner Samantha Fox is the breast of the bunch; that flu jabs give Dr Vernon

Coleman the needle; that henpecked factory worker Andre Gaillard set fire to his house because he was flaming mad; that brainy roadsweeper Ian Johnson's BA degree makes him a master of carts; that an overturned lorry which spilled tons of lard on the A1 was a fat lot of use; that a driving examiner too overweight to fasten his seat belt had an L of a tight squeeze; that certain Hollywood soap stars are all washed up; and that Prince Harry had a jelly good birthday party when young pals at his posh kindergarten sang 'FOUR he's a jolly good fellow'.

There will always be room for a really good pun or ingenious play on words in a headline (e.g. the *People*'s THEY'RE GUARDING THE CHANGE AT BUCKINGHAM PALACE on a story about royal thrift), which is where the pun started its long and mainly undistinguished career. There is hardly any place for it in the text. In either case, the story has to be of a very particular type to warrant tricks with words, and the tricks have to be good ones. Automatic punning is a tedious schoolboy game which must leave the reader feeling as he would if he switched on his TV and found the presenters playing ping-pong while reading the News at Ten.

So puns and wordplay are to be avoided – but they are especially to be avoided when:

1. They are out of date. THE DAILY SKETCHER was the headline on a *Times* feature about a freelance court artist. Its allusion is to the *Daily Sketch* newspaper which has been defunct since 1971.

2. They are unjustified. A *Sunday Times* interview

with a senior sub-editor on the *Sun* quotes his best headline, on a story about frogs being killed while crossing the road, as HALT! MAJOR TOAD AHEAD. Very good: but frogs (*rana temporaria),* while amphibian, are not toads (*bufo vulgaris*).

3. They are lame. WATER BAD IDEA, on a *Daily Star* story about an angler chased by wasps, was a very bad idea.

4. They are really excruciating, like the *Sun's* headline on a story of a cockney TV personality's plan to celebrate his wedding day with fish and chips: HERE COMES THE FRIED, or the *News of the World's* schoolboyish HELLO, WHAT'S ALL THIS EAR? on an account of how an angry prisoner was all ears after he got his head stuck in a cell door.

5. They are inappropriate. BLOW ME! was a funny headline for the *Daily Mirror* to put on a report of a hurricane. But since it killed many people, and the story contained a quote from the Jamaican Prime Minister, 'This is like Hiroshima', it was not funny ha-ha.

6. They are obvious. A comedian going into hospital is bound to have the nurses *in stitches.* He did – in at least three papers.

7. They are obscure. KING OF THE MILD FRONTIER was the *Guardian* headline on a profile of Eddie Shah [founder of Today newspaper in 1986]. A careful reading of the text yielded some small justification for MILD but none at all for FRONTIER.

8. They are laboured, like Mr Pooter's puns in *The Diary of a Nobody* ('I'm *'fraid* this shirt is *frayed!'*). Mr

Pooter must have been subbing on the *Daily Express* the night a gossip paragraph about Prince Andrew's photographic activities inspired SNAPPER ANDY SHOULDN'T BE BROW BEATON.

9. They do not make sense, e.g. a *Mail on Sunday* caption on a picture of a woman holding up the only fork available in a railway dining car: GOING FOR A PRONG. The play is on the title of a defunct TV show about antiques, 'Going for a Song'. Neither singing nor antiques came into the story, unless one counts the age of the joke.

10. They are ancient. Over half a century after it first thought of the pun, the *Daily Mirror* is still putting the headline PURRFECT ENDING! on items about cats which came within a whisker of using up all their nine lives.

Quote unquote

Except where obligatorily wrapped around passages of reported speech or introduced as typographical crossed fingers to ward off libel actions, inverted commas are haphazardly used in newspapers.

A piece about currency controls says that they cost a fortune to *'police'* (in quotes) and that they *strangle* (not in quotes) business.

There is inconsistency here. The first word is in quotes because we don't mean *police* literally (or we think we don't, but the *Concise Oxford* gives 'v.t.... control'). But we don't mean *strangle* literally, either. So we should say either:

> They cost a fortune to 'police'. They 'strangle' business.

or:

> They cost a fortune to police. They strangle business.

As always, the least fussy version is best.

Here is an example of quotes being used for all sorts of different reasons – not all of them completely justified:

> Doctors have been given the go-ahead to prescribe the controversial 'morning after' Pill.
>
> It is not foolproof, and it is to be used only as an 'emergency measure' – for instance, to prevent a rape victim becoming pregnant…
>
> But it MIGHT NOT WORK, warns the Department of Health.
>
> And, if it fails, an embryo baby could be deformed.
>
> The 'green light' for the method is given in the latest edition of the Health Department's book on birth control…

Morning after seems to have been given quotes here because the (usually hyphenated) expression *morning-after Pill* is not yet deemed to be in general use.

It is not clear why *emergency measure* is in quotes. It is not an unusual phrase or saying. The words are not being used ironically. No one is being quoted (or perhaps they are? But the paragraph doesn't credit the source).

Green light is presumably in quotes because it is an expression borrowed from popular usage – slang, almost. But the newspapers are full of examples of everyday language (or if they are not, they should be). If they were to put them all in inverted commas, their pages would look like flypapers.

In the one place where quotation marks might have strengthened the story – on the warning from the Department of Health – they are not used, although even if the quote is indirect speech or a summary, they would have been justified. But at least this particular paragraph follows what should be a general principle. Inverted commas clutter up the narrow columns of newspapers and should be used as little as possible.

Where they are used, they should be used consistently:

500,000 HOMEBUYERS
'GAZUMPED' LAST YEAR

About 500,000 homebuyers were gazumped last year...

In that report, the *Daily Telegraph*'s right sub-editorial hand did not seem to know what its left was doing. Or was *gazumped* deemed all right to be tucked away in the text but too vernacular a word to adorn a headline without the disclaimer of quotation marks?

Ramboism

Rambo is to the popular press what Dennis the Menace is to the *Beano* comic: an indispensable, larger-than-life figure who if he had not already been invented would have to be given existence. Splash subs embraced him from the start – probably because he sounds so much like one of the soccer stars whose nicknames adorn their sports pages; certainly because like Robbo, Dobbo *et al.*, the name is short enough to be set in a type size worthy of being held in reserve for the outbreak of World War III.

It is impossible to compute how many permutations on the theme of RAMBO BOY ON RAMPAGE, or, in the absence of a *rampage boy* as he is often called in the text (one half expects to see the headline RAMPAGE BOY ON RAMBO), the number of RAMBO GUNS CLAMPDOWN variations there have been since the Hungerford Massacre pioneered this class of story. RAMBO MUM has had less exposure: she turns out to be Sylvester Stallone's mother.

But Ramboism in newspapers is not confined to exploitation of the screen character's macho name. It has become an editorial style. Swaggering, even bullying, Rambo-type headlines, once restricted to the venerable COME OFF IT! abound – particularly in the sports pages, the principle seemingly being that in the best-selling equation of sex 'n' violence, the sex should be in the front half of the paper and the violence mainly at the back.

Unlike the RAMBO RAMPAGE formula, however, this type of headline does not require an actual rampage, or even the hint of one, to call itself into existence.

Thus WE'LL STUFF YOU! straddled two pages of the *Sunday People*, embracing an interview with the England soccer captain on one page and Fred Trueman's cricket commentary on the other, but without any indication as to who proposed to stuff whom. The text did not help. On neither page was the headline quoted or even justified, unless 'We're coming to win the European championship' on the one hand, or 'Botham can still be the best no. 4 bat in England if he has a mind to' on the other, can be construed as 'We'll stuff you!'

SHUT YOUR BIG MOUTH, LEWIS! headlined a *Daily Star* interview with a 'top athlete' on the subject of his rival. No such words, or anything like them, appear in the interview, its most inflammatory quote being 'I think people are getting fed up with him continually coming out with innuendoes about drugs and pointing the finger at others.'

The *Daily Star* also had STICK IT! on a story about a 'golden girl javelin ace' who felt that despite winning an Olympics gold medal she had been treated like a second-class athlete. 'Stick it!' turns out to be sub-editorial shorthand for 'The British vest is all very nice and it's nice to feel you're out there for your country – but it doesn't mean anything to me now.'

UP YOURS! was the main headline on a *Daily Mirror* cricket story whose subsidiary heading was *Gooch & Co. say no to Boks*. The only quotes from Gooch & Co. were: 'I haven't received my England contract from the Test and County Cricket Board yet. But when I do I will be signing it. And wherever England go this winter I will be available'; and 'I'll be signing my contract as soon as I receive it. And I'm convinced all the other players will do the same.' Who exclaimed 'Up yours!', and to whom, remains a mystery.

BRUNO: I'M GUTTED was a *Sun* back-page headline. *Gutted* has been given much exposure in the tabloids since it replaced *sick as a parrot* in the sporting vocabulary. But it was not used by Mr Bruno on this particular occasion.

But the misleading Rambo headline is by no means entirely confined to the back pages, for all that sports desks seem to be heavily influenced by soccer violence. STUFF IT, MA'AM! cried the headline over a *News of the World* exclusive on why 'royal cook Marje turns down £90-a-week job'. But royal cook Marje had said no such thing. It is a case of the *News of the World* putting words into its own mouth: 'Convent cook Marjorie Lonnen has told the Queen Mum to stuff a plum job in her London home.'

The case against the Rambo headline, however, is not only that it promises more than it delivers. That is not entirely a novelty in headlines. It is that it comes lunging out of its corner with short, sharp, aggressive words intended to hit the reader in the mouth, thus giving a new dimension to the expression *punchy* which is what all self-respecting tabloids would claim to be. One imagines a bench of sub-editors in string vests with tattooed arms and shaven heads and a six-pack of lager within reach.

On 30 June 1988, the *Daily Mirror* scored a first – and possibly an own goal – by introducing the word ARSE into its front page in 72-point capitals, in the headline YOU SMART ARSE KRAUT! This was a direct quote attributed to the Australian tennis player Pat Cash, directed against Boris Becker. Unlike the other examples quoted it was completely substantiated by the supporting story. Indeed the *Mirror*, having committed itself to this pioneering splash, could have had a field day with the gist of the quote in full, since what Cash appears to have said was that Becker was a 'f---ing smart arse Kraut'.

Doubtless such a day will come. The unacceptable backside of the *Mirror*'s front page, consciously or not, was a response to the Rambo headlines in the *Sun* in particular and to a lesser extent the *Daily Star* and the *News of the World*. BASTARDS! on IRA and other terrorist stories has become so commonplace a *Sun* response that it may as well be kept permanently set in type. LOCK UP THE BLOODY IRA BASTARDS! shouts a *News of the World* leader. WHY THE DOGS HAD TO DIE is the headline on the *Sun*'s Page One Opinion ('The *Sun* speaks its mind') on the deaths of three IRA terrorists shot by the SAS in Gibraltar. A few days later another *Sun* leader has LET THEM ROT on bank robbers who took hostages, while the *Daily Star* offers SAS RUB OUT IRA RATS, and, on the impending death of Emperor Hirohito, LET THE BASTARD ROT IN HELL!

It is questionable whether rabble-rousing is among the proper functions of the newspaper headline; but that question is for others to ask. The question posed here is whether Ramboism is effective. The answer is that the return on over-excited sub-editing can only be a diminishing one. As with what a *Guardian* writer had dubbed 'bonking journalism' (see SEX ROMPS), the reader quickly becomes immune to shock (especially if it is the shock of discovering that the words in big black capital letters are nothing to do with the story), and the dose has to be stepped up. Hence the giant leap for newspapermankind between COME OFF IT! and YOU SMART ARSE KRAUT!

Tabloid journalism should speak street language but it should not get its language from street walls. Good headlines are distinguishable from graffiti.

Rank and file

In the armed forces, other ranks are often identified by their trade or calling - Rifleman Jones, Cook-corporal Smith, Signalman Brown, Telegraphist Black. Even Boy Robinson.

The practice has been adopted with gusto by Fleet Street.

On a single (and typical) day, the following roll-call, in order of appearance, could have been taken in the *Daily Mirror* lines (and the other two red top tabloids could have mustered matching forces):

Blushing bride Diane Gittins
Former *Sun* writer Tim Ewbank
TV chat show host Terry Wogan

Greenwich Council Works Department foreman Fred
    Vaughan
Soccer boss Brian Clough
Actor Peter O'Toole
Gasman Nigel Day
Charmer star Nigel Havers
Sex-in-the-shower scandal MP Ron Brown
Pensioner Percy Curtis
Pupil Lindsay Lonergan, 16
Record-breaker Sebastian Coe
Sussex Chief Constable Reginald Birch
Brave businessman Alan Waller
Eurythmics star Dave Stewart
Cheeky pop star Howard Jones
Queen star Roger Taylor
Headmistress Josephine Donaldson
NUT regional branch secretary Tom Trafford
Model agency boss Yvonne Paul
Top model Linda Lusardi
Spandau Ballet star Gary Kemp
Shamed TV evangelist Jimmy Swaggart
Impressionist Rory Bremner
Manchester United defender Paul McGrath
England manager Bobby Robson
Irish keeper Gerry Peyton
Former Nottingham Forest goalkeeper Hans van
    Breukelen
Benfica goalkeeper Louro Silvino
Walsall striker David Kelly

Walking-on parts such as Premiers, Chancellors,
Ministers and Shadow Spokesmen have been
omitted for reasons of space. Several colourful
characters – notably cockney comic Jim Davidson,

Jagger girl Jade, ice-cool actress Nyree Dawn Porter, jailed jockey Lester Piggott, and Fergie nanny Alison Wardley – were to be found in adjacent issues of the paper.

The list is admittedly only just over half as long as the one turned out by the *Mirror* for the original version of this manual. But it is still too long. The *Daily Mail*, on the same day, managed to get by with barely a dozen names prefixed with potted biographies.

While there can be nothing in principle against the practice of cramming as much information as possible into the shortest space, this is one of those areas where an accepted convention becomes tedious and irritating when overdone. Putting a comma after the descriptive noun – *a book written by British author, Alan Friedman* – does not help, although it may make the sub handling the copy feel he is raising its literary tone.

Besides being tiresome the convention can also, on occasion, seem faintly absurd, as when a reader's letter refers (or is made to refer) to *Cleveland Council's ruling Labour Group's disciplinary action against social services director Mike Bishop and abuse consultant Sue Richardson*, or when a fellow comedian is quoted as saying that *overweight comic Les Dawson has been overworking*.

A curious side product of the name-tag industry is the growing tendency, particularly in headlines, to identify persons in the news either by what makes them newsworthy, as *coma boy, death-fall teacher, desert-horror hubby, sex-ban star, tax-tangle comic, love-tangle rock star, stab dad, sex-storm barmaid, kidnap Briton, plunge mum*; or, more obscurely, by some event or object associated with their news-worthiness – *holiday girl, rhino trek man, bridge man, crossbow girl, rugby boot boy.*

The *Daily Telegraph*, for reasons best known to its chief sub, is particularly partial to this kind of labelling. But it is the Brighton *Evening Argus* which takes the medal for obscurity with the headline CRASH! IT'S A REAL LIVE SHOCKER FOR TELLY JOAN. Who telly Joan? The first five paragraphs tell how a woman leapt for her life when a neighbour's car reversed into her home. The sixth paragraph justifies the headline, or thinks it does: 'Joan said: "I am lucky to be alive. I was watching telly at the back of the lounge when… "'

It is sometimes difficult to see what principle is being followed in allocating descriptive prefixes to names in the news. How is it decided that, on the same page, Delhi science student Kapil Dev should appear as *Kapil Dev, a science student from Delhi*, while in the report of a Gillette Cup match between Lancashire and 'Championship leaders Essex', Frank Hayes, who was far from fit, should appear as *far-from-fit Frank Hayes*?

What is not so difficult to see is why pages unencumbered by an abundance of thumb-nail-biography name-tags are less of a headache to read than pages over-endowed with them. The journalist who writes of a *missing teenage MG driver* instead of a *vanished MG girl* has tried harder, and so made his meaning clearer. But clarity is not always the issue: the football report bespattered with *striker* Smith, *keeper* Jones, *defender* Robinson (the sports pages are a breeding-ground for labels) may be a model of clarity. Yet those sports writers, and there are several of them around, who make a point of not identifying every player as if his position were his rank tend to be more readable than their name-tagging colleagues.

Says who?

The place for the passive voice is Whitehall, not Fleet Street.

> It is thought that Wednesday's Derby at Epsom could be the last to be shown by the BBC.

It is thought by whom?

> LWT are said to be particularly pleased with the Derby contract...

Who said it?

The active voice is preferable for newspapers because it answers questions. The passive voice often sounds as if it had something to hide. It can also waste time:

> Petrol is running out and booze is being put into fuel tanks.

By whom? By Brazilians, it says in the second paragraph. Then why not say it in the first paragraph? Answer: because of the national newspaper principle that what happens is more interesting than where it happens. But is the principle infallible? The second paragraph reads:

> So desperate is the world oil crisis that in Brazil they are putting alcohol in their cars.

This repeats all the information we've just been given in the first paragraph, but makes a livelier job of it because the story now involves people.

The active voice is best even if the source has to be anonymous or general (*Police think* for *It is thought*, *Sources believe* for *It is believed that*). If the source is the cuttings library, then the less said about what is said to have been said, the better.

Exceptions… *It was claimed yesterday* in court story intros. This shorthand saves words and keeps the paper out of trouble. And *It was revealed* may protect a reporter's contacts.

Screamers!

Exclamation marks should be used in exclamatory headlines (HAMMERED!), in reported speech ('Was my face red!') in titles of films etc ('Oliver!'), in editorial ejaculations ('Come off it!'), and as little as possible anywhere else.

The exclamation mark is an aid to good English. It is not a prop for bad writing.

A sentence that falls flat without an exclamation mark is a flat sentence. The exclamation mark will not inject drama into it. It must be re-cast.

An exclamation mark supposedly pointing up the irony of a particular passage is trying to do the job of H. L. Mencken's invented typeface ironics, which slope the opposite way to italics. But the passage should do its own signposting, otherwise it is ambiguous.

Exclamation marks cannot tell the reader that the story is funny. The most they can tell him is that it was meant to be funny.

Even in headlines, which is their proper place in newspapers (particularly sports headlines), exclamation marks are seldom necessary, except to draw attention to a bad pun or as makeweight where the headline was slightly shy of its required width. A trawl of a day's batch of national newspapers turned up twenty-four exclamation marks in the red-top tabloids, one each in the *Mail* and the *Express*, none in the *Guardian, Independent, Financial Times* or *The*

Times, and two in the *Daily Telegraph.* None of them served the slightest purpose except the *Telegraph's* two, which were on successive leaders headed *O Tempora!* and *O Mores!*

Sexism

The sex barrier in Fleet Street is very clearly defined. Barbara Smith is Miss Smith or Barbara Smith in *The Times*, the *Independent* and the *Daily Telegraph*, Smith in the *Guardian*, Babs in the *Daily Mirror*, and busty Babs in the *Sun* and *Daily Star*.

As for Barbara Smith's mother, Mrs Bessie Smith, she is Mrs in all the text papers and Mum Bess or Babs' Mum Bess in the tabloids.

It is doubtful whether this great divide is ever to be bridged, since an excessive chumminess is the hallmark of the tabloids, while the text papers are on first-name terms with their subjects only in the occasional feature interview. Furthermore, the taloids, and to some extent the other popular papers, still live in a world of *housewives* (or *mums*) and *career girls* (both the *Daily Mirror* and the *Daily Mail* contrived to carry an item on the misadventures of a career girl without ever mentioning what her career was). Women professionals are women first and professionals after – Dr Barbara Smith, however senior, is Dr Babs or at best Dr Barbara. As discussed under ADJECTIVES, her name is likely to be prefixed by some vague complimentary description – *attractive, brunette, vivacious*.

Page three girls are at least sometimes balanced with page five or page seven 'fellas'. A sense of balance between the sexes elsewhere in the paper would not go amiss.

Sex romps

Fleet Street's sex life goes back well into the nineteenth century, when the *Police Gazette* would devote closely packed column after closely packed column to the divorce scandals of the day. When heavy restrictions were placed on the reporting of divorce cases, the *News of the World* scoured the criminal courts for stories with a strong sex angle. The old *Sunday Dispatch* introduced the spicy serial with such titles as FOREVER AMBER. Then came an era of exposures of sundry 'vice dens' by reporters who made an excuse and left. Then a market in 'sizzling confessions' – the titillating ghosted memoirs of 'sex sirens' with mirrors on their bedroom ceilings followed by rather juicier recollections of their disgruntled maids, chauffeurs or gardener-lovers in the Chatterley tradition. What the *Guardian* was to christen 'bonk journalism' had by now laid down its roots.

So there is nothing new in Fleet Street's obsession with sex., whereby – for instance – the refusal of police to say whether a strangulation victim has been sexually assaulted merits the *Sun* headline GIRL'S SEX DEATH IN STREAM. In becoming more explicit and 'daring' down the years, it is only following life itself. What is new is the crass form of language employed in the endless Bimbo-tells-all and rentboy-spills-the-beans tabloid exclusives. And it is with newspaper language, rather than the vagaries of newspaper morality, that we are here concerned.

On one level Fleet Streets' vocabulary of expressions for sexual activity is as comparatively coy and euphemistic as in those gaslit days when men about town engaged in dalliances with ladies of the night in houses of assignation. Now saucy studs have sex romps with topless hostesses in private massage clubs. Steamy nights of passion are indulged in with dream lovers by blonde beauties, while teenage temptresses run away from top schools with sexy sirs. It is still the bland, pap-provocation of the cheap novelettes with which the tabloids have always contrived to keep pace through the ages.

But on another level they have left Mills & Boon far behind. Three examples will suffice:

We had sex non-stop. We did it in front of the fire first, then as we were unpacking the shopping from Marks & Spencer he lifted me up onto the kitchen unit. He got a banana and used it on me before unzipping it and scoffing it down at the crucial moment.

We went back to my flat and he was the perfect gentleman at first. Then, just as he was leaving he asked me for a kiss – but we couldn't stop there.

I saw his credentials and thought my luck was really in. But it was all over in 30 seconds and I was left feeling very disappointed.

He wouldn't get onto the substitutes' bench compared with my other lovers.

He plied me with brandy, and brandy makes me randy. Then he nudged up and pecked my cheek.

He got really excited and we ended up in his bedroom. But he was so small, and in 30 seconds it was all over.

I got up, found my knickers in the sitting-room and went home.

Afterwards he apologized for his 'chipolata' and that's what I called him.

The disappointing lover's name being Rod, this last story was headed CHIPOLATA LOVER – SEX PEST MODEL'S BITTER BLAST AT HER SMALL ROD. Not even the bedroom is sacrosanct when the tabloids spot the possibility of a bad pun.

Alan Rusbridger noted in the *Guardian* about the

first of these examples that it is written in 'Penthouse Gothic, the particular style employed by the fantasy departments of the soft-core monthlies'. The other two examples are written in the same style – they may well have been written by the same hand – but if the object of soft-core is to arouse, they signally fail to do so. Like much of this type of material, with its banal euphemisms – *crucial moment, saw his credentials* – and unconscious insight into empty, shoddy lives, they make depressing reading. The last of these revelations continues, 'After we split, I went on holiday with another man. But all he did was lie on his bed and read about computers.' It is hardly the stuff of sexual fantasy. But perhaps the tabloids do secretly find sex a turn-off. A *Sun* headline, HYPNOTIST PUT PATIENTS UNDER FOR SEX ROMPS, perhaps says more about the *Sun* than about the case.

Tabloid editors would probably claim that their intention is to expose, not to excite. In which case they must often achieve their aim. A final quote from this particular stable, 'He has got a very small one and did absolutely nothing for me', adequately sums up the new sleaze.

There would be utterly no point in discussing how this kind of stuff could be better written. It could only be improved by not being written at all. No one is forced to write it, any more than anyone is forced to read it. Those who care about journalism can only hope, as one routinely sordid set of revelations follows another, that it will be subject to the law of diminishing return. (Some of the text papers, incidentally, are not above dipping their toes into the murky sex romps pond, usually with some such holier-than-thou aside as: 'The tabloids, of course, had a field day.')

Meanwhile, what should concern us here is how the influence of the sleazy sex romps sub-culture is seeping through into other pages, as in SWIM ACE TELLS GIRL 'NO NOOKIE', which was how the *Daily Star* chose to interpret the decision of an 'Olympic golden boy' and his girlfriend not to get in touch with one another until after the Games. From a *News of the World* headline on a gangster's confessions, KILLING GAVE ME AN ORGASM, to a gratuitous footnote on a *Sun* story about a man who swallowed his TV set's miniature remote control unit with the result that when he hiccups it changes channels, 'It could be worse, Vern – if you lived in Britain, every time you broke wind you'd get Newsnight', and the red top press (with the notable exception of the *Daily Mirror*) gets bluer by the day. Perhaps tabloid editors believe their readers are unshockable. At any rate the *Sun* ran a story about how 'millions of Radio 2 listeners were shocked' when they heard a 'cheeky radio presenter' say apropos an athlete's hopes, 'The poor guy must have been going up and down like a bride's nightie, as they say in Oldham.' The *Sun*'s 36-point headline was UP AND DOWN LIKE A BRIDE'S NIGHTIE. Either BBC2's millions of listeners have more delicate sensibilities than the *Sun*'s millions of readers, and their paths do not cross, or the *Sun* was having it both ways.

While there is no reason why the budding journalist should be expected to carry Max Miller's gag book in his pocket, there is of course a world of difference between sleaziness and what the tabloids like to call 'cheekiness'. They were ever cheeky but never sleazy. It is a relief to turn from the sad little world of a sex pest model and her small Rod to the healthier activities of 'sexy sailor girls who joined a crew of lusty lads for a voyage around the world – and FOUR of them ended up pregnant'. The *News of the World* headline is GIRLS JOLLY ROGERED! The *Sun*, for its part, on a report that the contents of sandwiches can give away 'your saucy bedroom secrets', put up the headline FANCY A ROLL, LUV? This is back in the footsteps of Donald McGill. They may lead us to the quicksands of FACETIOUSNESS but it is a more bracing route than the one that ends up at the sewage outlet.

Stagger off

Sums of money, percentages, weights, heights, depths, lengths, numbers, measurements by volume, temperatures, distances, prices, and so on, do not stagger.

Where *staggering* (going unsteadily as if about to fall; shaking conviction; giddiness as in horses and cattle disease) is supposed to convey *astonishing*, it no longer does. The word is worn out.

Supernumeraries

Super as a prefix still has a certain amount of tread left in it. *Superbrat*, though a little worn by now, was original and evocative. *Superpit* was a good shorthand way of describing the new modern mines. But *superstar*, as applied to anyone who has made a few films or CDs, has been so freely endowed that a super-super category, *megastar*, has had to be invented. *Supermums* and *superdads* must have had their day by now, but they still make regular appearances in the tabloids. (The *People* missed the opportunity to upgrade the mother of an incredible fifty-nine babies to the status of *megamum*.)

Super can still be useful – if new uses are found for it.

Tabloidese

Tabloidese, that tough-guy, hat-on-the-back-of-the-head talk that makes newspapers sound like James Cagney (*rap, probe, bid, swoop, axe*) was devised to accommodate the largest type to the smallest page.

Partly inspired by the back numbers department of the New York *Daily News* (a newspaper which still uses a logo of a squeeze-bulb plate camera on its masthead) and by old Death Row movies, it is essentially a made-up language, a kind of primitive Esperanto where nouns, verbs and adjectives are interchangeable. So long as readers are well-versed in this Esperanto, it is a useful – indeed an essential – headline aid. But is it always comprehensible? Do those hard-boiled newspaper cynics who habitually ask, 'Will our readers in Wigan understand this?' ever ask themselves if the reader from Wigan (or the Bronx) can follow, for instance, TORCH BOY SET ABLAZE BY GANG?

Set ablaze by gang is clear enough, but what is a *torch boy*? It can only be (as the copy confirms) a boy who has been set ablaze. So if the Esperanto headline were translated into something approaching English, it would read ABLAZE BOY SET ABLAZE BY GANG.

Is the headline TRIPLE LOVE-SNATCH BOY IS HUNTED any relation to TORMENT OF A LOVE-TUG MUM? Do we all understand, without reference to the accompanying text, that a *triple love-*

snatch boy is one who has been seized by his father, from his mother, for the third time? Do we have some idea of what a *love-tug mum* is? If so, does it confuse us or enlighten us when in the first paragraph of the love-tug mum's story she becomes a *love-tug wife*?

Perhaps further discussion of the uses and abuses of this peculiar language could be helped by a 'Concise Dictionary of Tabloidese':

About to – *poised*
Anger – *fury*
Annoyance – *outrage*
Argument – *storm*
Arrangement – *deal*
Attempt – *bid*
Avoid – *shun*
Bad luck – *jinx, curse*
Campaign – *crusade*
Cancel – *axe, scrap*
Confiscate – *grab*
Connection – *link*
Contest – *battle*
Control – *crackdown, clampdown*
Controversy - *row, turmoil*
Criticize – *slam, blast, hit out*
Development – *move*
Difficulty – *snag, hurdle*
Disagreement – *clash*
Dismissed – *dumped, axed*
Division – *split*
Draw attention to – *alert*
Drive – *blitz*

Encourage – *boost*
Error – *blunder, bungle*
Exclude – *bar, ban*
Expel - *boot out, kick out*
Fail to attend – *snub*
Fatal fall – *death plunge*
Fire – *blaze*
Happening – *drama*
Hurry – *dash*
Impose - *slap*
Internal dispute – *civil war*
Likely to – *set to*
Mystery – *riddle*
Non-participants – *rebels*
Patrol – *vigil*
Possibility – *threat*
Promise – *vow, pledge*
Proposal – *plan*
Question – *quiz*
Quarrel – *feud*
Raid – *swoop*
Reduce – *cut*
Reform – *shake-up*
Relief – *mercy*
Replace – *oust*
Reprove – *rap*
Request – *call*
Resign – *quit, storm out*
Restrict – *curb*
Rise – *soar*
Rivalry – *war*
Setback – *blow*
Sex – *sex romps*
Shocked – *rocked*

Support – *rally*
Traffic jam – *road chaos*
Vital – *key*

It will be noted that in nearly every case (the most notable exception being *sex romps* for sex), the tabloid word is shorter than its definition, which is as it should be. It is also usually harder – in many cases (*slam, hit back, clash, war*) to the point of downright belligerence. This is often where reality leaves off and something approaching RAMBOISM takes over. The great danger of tabloidese is that its macho approach combined with a highly developed sense of the melodramatic can lead it to exaggerate.

In tabloid terms an attempt may always be a *bid*, a connection a *link* and a fatal fall a *death plunge*, but is an argument invariably a *storm,* a contest a *battle,* a surprise a *shock* – and indeed is a drama always a drama? CHARLES IN FILM SNUB DRAMA promises much but delivers little. It turns out that in initially refusing to boycott a film (the headline, incidentally, suggests the opposite), Prince Charles has incurred the displeasure of one or two people whose mildly reproving quotes form the burden of the story – a controversy, perhaps, but hardly the stuff of drama, and certainly not one that places him *at the centre of a bitter row* as the intro, in an attempt to support its own headline, would have it.

There will always be a demand for short bold words to fit big bold headlines. There is no reason why these should not be 'label' words, often found nowhere else in the language – a label, after all, is precisely what the headline is. But as any reputable patent medicine manufacturer would agree, a label must tell the consumer clearly what is in the bottle. If it doesn't, it is a case of either quackery, flimflam or incompetence.

But what of tabloidese 'label' words that – seemingly with the same territorial ambitions as PUNS – have slunk down from the headline to the text? What are they doing there? The average news story, after all, is not set in 144-point. True, space is always at a premium, but is it at such a premium that the reader must have his Tabloidese Dictionary at the ready?

> Doctors and ambulancemen were *slammed* yesterday...

Diesel train services are to be *axed* by British Rail in a desperate *bid* to save fuel...

A lonely old peer lured young girls into bed for *sex romps*...

A *call* to end a union *civil war* was made yesterday as a threat to *boot* electricians out of the TUC *loomed*...

A *blaze* superstore has told its *till girls*, 'Dump the money and run for your lives...'

It could be argued that most of these expressions have been used (over-used?) so often that the readers know exactly what they mean. Probably so, in the headline sense. But what, outside the headlines, is a *sex romp*? What is a *blaze superstore*? Who are *till girls*? Why, if these words are now so common, are they not in common use? Why do we not hear people at bus stops saying, 'Our Marlene used to be a till girl at that blaze superstore' or 'Did I tell you about young Fred being rapped after he slammed the boss? He thinks he's going to be axed'? Words that have never managed to get into the mainstream of the language are suspect as a means of popular communication.

They are, and remain, labels. They do not convey precise meanings. The reader looks at the label, opens the tin – and finds a tin of labels.

Tabloidese, furthermore, is essentially passive. In tabloid-land, *400 jobs face axe*. In real life, 400 may lose their jobs. Intended to be dramatic, tabloidese has a curiously deadening effect. *A pay war loomed last night* is not dramatic because it has all the ingredients of drama except the players – the story does not come to life until we know who is involved in it.

Sometimes it does not come to life even then. Two athletes who are *set for a head-on showdown* prove to be simply competing in the same event.

Tautology

The BBC's evening news committed these two tautologisms in the same bulletin: *mutual agreement* (as distinct from unilateral agreement?) and *strange phenomenon* (all phenomena, in the now widely accepted sense of something remarkable, are strange. However, style books which quote *strange coincidence* as tautology are wrong. It would be a coincidence if two Welshmen in the same room were called Jones, but not a very strange one.)

The BBC's news-gatherers are in good tautological company. It took only as many minutes to find the following half-dozen examples in one day's crop of papers:

A *major* nuclear *disaster* could have been sparked off...

... who *died* of a *fatal* dose of heroin

... *equalized* the game to a 2-2 *draw*

... *kept it from* his friends that he was a *secret* drinker

Dirty Den has made up his mind *never to go back* to EastEnders, *finally severing his connection* with the soap

... a group for *one-parent single* mothers

Tautology is either unnecessary elaboration (the Inland Revenue's *white-collar* workers), pointless repetition (*pair* of twins), superfluous description (Europe's *huge* butter mountain), a needless appendage (weather *conditions*) or a self-cancelling proposition (He is either guilty or not guilty). Journalistically if not grammatically speaking, successive sentences or even paragraphs may be tautological, and often are:

> The dockers' jobs-for-life scheme is facing the axe.
> Mrs Thatcher is backing calls from Tory backbenchers for a repeal of the 40-year-old Dock Labour Act, which prevents dockers being sacked.

Either the first sentence could be omitted (or axed) and the last clause of the second sentence be re-worked to read '…which guarantees dockers a job for life'; or the sharper opening sentence could stand, and such additional information as is conveyed by the second sentence be accommodated in the body of the story (as indeed it already is – twice).

Tautology is not only a waste of words in a context where every word should count, it is also proof of slack workmanship. Sentences containing tautologisms have not been crafted, they have been slung together. How reliable, then, the reader is entitled to ask, are the facts they contain?

Even if the facts are impeccable, a sentence that has not had the repetitions sieved out of it can give the wrong impression to the unwary; the group for one-parent single mothers cited above could be a group for single mothers with only one parent each.

All the examples of tautology quoted could have been avoided had their perpetrators been in the habit of automatically screening their work with the question. 'What is the function of this word in this sentence?' When it comes to duplication for the sake of bolstering a weak story, that sort of thing – '*full* and *total* support' – is best left to trade union leaders and politicians.

None of the words italicized below are necessary:

> Pronounced there was more to come *later*
> Razed *to the ground*
> Battle lines are being drawn *up*
> Shunted *off* into the sidings
> Filled *up*
> Said he had nothing *further* to add
> Strike *action*

Redundant words merely clutter the page, as do unnecessary auxiliaries and conjunctions – *he said he was* is as clear as *he said that he was*. In most cases, *in many cases* is unnecessary – *Many parents had not been told*, not *In many cases, parents had not been told*. *Charges of a serious nature* or *serious character* are better pruned to *serious charges*.

But beware of pruning too zealously:

> Millions of Londoners are facing a hefty hike in bus and tube fares.
> London Regional Transport announced a 12.4 per cent increase in January.

No. They announced it in September. But what they announced was that *there would be* a 12.4 per cent increase in January.

The tops

Top, as meaning senior, highly placed, important, exclusive, etc., is a lazy word that does not earn its keep. Its purpose often seems to be to impress the reader rather than to inform.

Compare the degrees of topness of the following *top* people or institutions:

Top scientists

One of London's top schools (a London crammer's)

A top publisher (a publisher)

A top industry source (anonymous)

A top soccer club (Premier League)

A top college (a school in Kent)

Top Tory ministers (junior ministers)

Top cops

A top pop studio

A top producer

A top diplomat (a third secretary)

A top royal writer (Anthony Holden)

A top restaurant (which faced a grilling over its dirty kitchens)

A top car-maker

A top TV thriller writer (Roald Dahl)

A top police surgeon (who had sex romps)

A top jail

All these (and more) appeared in our top tabloids within a day or two of one another. Not that the text papers are by any means topless. *The Times* now translates the Headmasters' Conference as *headmasters of Britain's top schools.*

The description *top* is in some cases unnecessary, in others of doubtful suitability, and in yet others so vague as to be without any meaning. It can even be downright misleading. *Today* described a Guy's anaesthetist as a *top doctor* and then went on to quote his head of department – presumably an even more top doctor.

Top reached its peak in the *Daily Mirror's* revelation that a polo match was attended by 2,000 top people. As to what they were top of, or top at, the paper did not elaborate.

Top has become a reflex word. It has not been helped by the legions of top models who have graced the pages of the tabloids (though we may take it as a blessing that the punsters have not yet discovered any bottom models). It is too all-embracing to be accurate, and should be discouraged.

The weather-vane

Extremes of weather (i.e. when Britain sizzles or the BRRometer is below freezing point) always provide a good opportunity to test prevailing facetiousness levels.

The following reading, taken during a heat wave, shows puns and wordplay at dangerously near the contamination mark:

COOL IT! IT'S A BLOWN PHEWS

> Britain was on the boil again yesterday – but don't presume we're going to get into the hotspot habit.
>
> For weathermen warned that the phews has failed...

The previous day's weather headline –

RETURN OF THE PHEW

– had the merit of being less groan-inducing, but was let down by the intro, which had June bustin' out all over (song title: 1954) yet again. But it is interesting that all the PHEW variations, whether weak or witty (usually weak), depend for their effect on the reader's recollection of the greatest headline cliché of all time. PHEW! WHAT A SCORCHER! was worn so threadbare in its day that any reference to it is supposed to be a shared joke between newspaper and reader – a rare case of a trade choosing to remind the customers of its own shoddy workmanship. The PHEW joke has been so overdone that it has become a cliché born of a cliché.

Weather stories in general have always attracted a determinedly boisterous approach, partly because the British weather is commonly a subject of saloon-bar jocularity and partly because since only unusual weather is worth reporting, the round-up tends to be larger than life. (An excellent example appears under AND NOW.)

Temperatures *soar* (or *plunge*), Britain *swelters* (or *shivers*) – and *there's more to come, say the weathermen* (or: *But make the most of it, say the weathermen*). Allowing that it's the same story every year, this year's story does not necessarily have to read like a photocopy of last year's story.

What rot

National newspapers intending to flourish in the twenty-first century should not use expressions that belong to the eighteen-nineties.

But they do.

Royal Ascot stories ('THE BOUNDER WHO BARGED THE QUEEN. He may have looked like a toff in his top hat and tails. But, by George, the man was a cad') and public school stories ('I say, you chaps! Here's some jolly frightful news about Eton') must make readers wonder whether they are reading a modern daily paper or a back number of the *Magnet* (expired 1940).

P. G. Wodehouse and Frank Richards, both past their prime when their idiosyncratic prose first came to be commonly imitated in Fleet Street, and both long since dead, never pretended that they were reproducing real-life speech patterns. Richards borrowed from Kipling's *Stalky & Co.* (1899) and Wodehouse took many of his 'Man-about-town' expressions from W. S. Gilbert (born 1836).

The following expressions survive in reprinted editions of the dead authors mentioned, and in the news columns of contemporary popular newspapers:

All, dash it
Ass, prize
Aunt, my giddy
Aunt, my sainted

Beasts, those
Blighter
Bounder
Brigade, top-hat-and-spats
Cad
Chappies, those Eton
Chaps, look here you
Crikey
Die, laugh my dear, I thought I'd
Deuced
Escutcheon, blot on the old
Fellows, I say you
Frightful, jolly
Gad, by
George, by
Gosh, golly
Gumdrops, golly
Ho, tally
Ho, what
It, hang
Jape
Jeeves, I say
Jolly, how awfully
Jove, bai
Know, doncher
Lark, what a
Lor', good
Nerve, what a bally
Pip, pip
Priceless
Really, oh
Rotters
Rot, what absolute
Shame, dashed

Show, bad
Show, good
Sir, gad
Spiffin'
Stars, oh my
Thick, I say chaps it's a bit
Toff
Whacko
What, eh
What, what
Wheeze, I say chaps here's a
Yaroo

Which is that?

Which and *that* are regularly confused, in the mistaken belief that they are always interchangeable.

An over-simple definition, which at any rate will serve to cover those areas of meaning where the confusion is more likely to be found, is:

That defines.
Which informs.

(*That* should be used without a comma. The clause introduced by *which* is usually contained within commas or preceded by one.)

The difference illustrated:

'The piece *that* the editor jumped up and down on is in the wastepaper basket.' This assumes that we already know about the editor's impetuous reaction, which is mentioned only so that we will know which piece is being talked about when we are given the news about it being thrown into the wastepaper basket.

But:

'The piece, *which* the editor jumped up and down on, is in the wastepaper basket.' This assumes that we already know which piece is being talked about, but we are being given *new information* about the editor's jumping-up-and-down activities.

In its complementary or introductory sense, *that* may often be omitted: the last sentence above could well read, without loss of sense or style, *This assumes we already know which piece,* etc. But reporters streamlining their sentences thus do so at their peril. A story entirely denuded of this little word – 'A survey showed women wanted equal treatment from hotels so they were not marked out as a target' - can give the impression of being written in cablese. The omission can also make the meaning unclear, as in this passage from a report in *Today,* a newspaper which appears to have taken a scythe to all its thats:

> Neighbour Mrs Jean Ashcroft said when her son arrived home from work yesterday and asked her how her day went she replied: 'Washing, ironing and neighbours held hostage by armed robbers.'

Good quote: shame about the sense. For the omission of *that* between *said* and *when* leads us to anticipate that what the lady said was to the reporter on the occasion of her son arriving home yesterday.

What is style?

The Times reported:

> The late Leonid Brezhnev suffered clinical death in January 1976, but was revived and ruled the Soviet Union in a virtual daze for six more years, a Soviet historian said yesterday.

The *Daily Mirror* reported:

> Former Kremlin chief Leonid Brezhnev ruled Russia for six years after 'dying', it was claimed yesterday.

It will be seen that there is little to choose between those two opening paragraphs. All the papers reported the news in pretty much the same straightforward way – except for the *Daily Star*, which after telling its readers that 'the fate of the world rested in the hands of a virtual zombie for six years', continued:

> He became what cynics have dubbed... the Red Cabbage.
> And that left corrupt officials who surrounded him in a pickle.

The interpolation of a weak joke into a serious news story is so inappropriate that it can only be described as oafish. Often, in its brash way, the *Daily Star* shows flair. On this occasion its sense of style utterly deserted it.

Good newspaper style does not only mean writing seriously about serious matters. Bringing a light touch to a lighthearted story requires the same sure touch. This is a fair example of *Daily Mirror* style:

Bachelor Stephen Howe really has his hands full running his own home.

He even turned down a free trip to the Continent because it would interfere with his housework.

The refusal angered his bosses, who had asked him to represent them at a scientific conference in Brussels.

Stephen, 29, said: 'Spending time away from home creates a backlog of housework, gardening and laundry.'

His bosses at Stone Platt Fluid Fire, Dudley, West Midlands, were amazed.

Company chairman Nathan Myers pointed out that Stephen was the only man capable of telling the conference about research he had been doing.

And Mr Myers went out of his way to eliminate any fears Stephen might have about the trip.

Frightened of flying? he asked Stephen.

No problem. We'll send you by sea.

Reluctant to spend two days away from home?

No problem. We'll make it a one-day trip.

But Stephen was adamant, and came up with a string of other reasons for not going. Such as...

- **I don't possess a decent suit.**
- **Foreign food upsets me.**
- **I haven't got a passport.**

- **I would have to buy a suitcase.**

Eventually Mr Myers got tough. Either you go to Brussels, he said – or you're fired.

Stephen, who owns a terraced house on a luxury estate in Wolverhampton, stuck to his guns.

He took Mr Myers to a Birmingham industrial tribunal alleging wrongful dismissal.

And the judgement went against Stephen – the houseproud bachelor who polished off his job.

Apart from the *really* blemish in the intro (see OH, REALLY?), and the fall from grace in the last sentence where the lure of the pun becomes to strong, the report is free of the cloying facetiousness that usually coats this type of story like melted toffee. Again we have a story straightforwardly told. The humour of the tale emerges without digging the reader in the ribs. It is well shaped. And for once italics, bold type and blobs are put to constructive use: they help the narrative along, as well as eliminating an excessive clutter of quotation marks.

One more example (of many available). A picture of Frank Sinatra playing chess with (and losing to) the world champion Anatoly Karpov was a ripe opportunity for Ol' Blue Eyes jests or chess jokes, had the *Mirror* wanted to stay on the familiar tracks. Instead, the headline had Sinatra saying, NICE MOVE, WISE GUY, NOW LET'S HEAR YOU SING. Not a pun in sight. That too is good newspaper style.

What is this style? Why do some stories, captions and headlines have it and others not? It would be fruitless to try to define it – as Fats Waller said when asked for a definition of jazz, 'Lady, if you have to ask, I can't tell you.' Obviously it demands flair, plus professionalism – two commodities that have never been in short supply in popular journalism. It demands experience, a quality that may be taken for granted in Fleet Street. For the rest, it consists simply of choosing a handful of words from the half a million or so samples available, and arranging them in the best order. Neither this manual nor any other can show anyone how to do that, but for those who wish to be reminded of the ground rules of what they now do by instinct, the following notes may be useful.

Use specific words (*red and blue*) not general ones (*brightly coloured*).

Use concrete words (*rain, fog*) rather than abstract ones (*bad weather*).

Use plain words (*began, said, end*) not college-educated ones (*commenced, stated, termination*).

Use positive words (*he was poor*) not negative ones (*he was not rich* – the reader at once wants to know, how not rich was he?).

Use the active voice (*police took no action*) not the passive voice (*no action was taken*).

Don't overstate: *fell* is starker than *plunged*.

Don't lard the story with emotive or 'dramatic' words (*astonishing, staggering, sensational, shock*).

Avoid non-working words that cluster together like derelicts (*but for the fact that, the question as to whether, there is no doubt that*).

Don't use words thoughtlessly. (*Waiting* ambulances don't rush victims to hospital. Waiting ambulances wait. Meteors fall, so there can be no *meteoric* rise.)

Don't use auxiliaries or conditionals (*was, might, would, should, may,* etc.) unless you have to. (*Mrs Thatcher is a political Florence Nightingale,* not *Mrs Thatcher* might be termed *a political Florence Nightingale.*)

Don't use unknown quantities (*very, really, truly, quite.* How much is *very*?).

Never qualify absolutes. A thing cannot be *quite impossible, glaringly obvious* or *most essential,* any more than it can be *absolutely absolute.*

Don't use wrong prepositions. (Check them for sense: we may *agree on* this point; you may *agree with* this opinion; he may *agree to* this proposal.)

Don't use jargon, clichés, puns, elegant or inelegant variations, or inexact synonyms (BRAVE WIFE DIED SAVING HER SON is wrong; wife is not a synonym for mother).

Use short sentences, but not all of the same length.

A succession of one-clause sentences is monotonous and wearying.

Avoid elaborate construction. Take the

sentence to pieces and re-cast it – probably as two sentences.

If a sentence reads as if it has something wrong with it, it has something wrong with it. *Whether you are motoring to see Mum, play trains in a railway museum or take in a stately home, this long Spring weekend can bring agony and death* is technically correct, but ugly.

Don't vary your rhythms for the sake of it. *He was not ill, and neither was he poor* is unnecessary variation. But there is a dramatic unity in *He was not ill. He was not poor.*

Even in a chronological narrative, the story should not start before it begins. *John Smith was really looking forward to his dinner* starts too early; the reader wants the dinner. Compare this with the opening of a short story by O. Henry: *So I went to the doctor.* A whole paragraph has happened offstage, and the reader is plunged straight into the action.

Words are facts. Check them (spelling and meaning) as you would any other.

Unlike every manual on style ever prepared, this one has reached its last pages without quoting the King James Bible as an example of how English may be written at its best. The omission will now be put right, but indirectly.

In his 1946 essay 'Politics and the English Language', George Orwell takes this passage from Ecclesiastes:

> I returned, and saw under the sun, that the race is not to the swift, nor the battle to the strong, neither yet bread to the wise, nor yet riches to men of understanding, nor yet favour to men of skill; but time and chance happeneth to them all.

He disembowels it, stuffs it with sawdust, and re-presents it as 'officialese':

> Objective consideration of contemporary phenomena compels the conclusion that success or failure in competitive activities exhibits no tendency to be commensurate with innate capacity, but that a considerable element of the unpredictable must invariably be taken into account.

This is the kind of Whitehall gobbledegook that the tabloids have lampooned over the years. Yet how, sixty years after Orwell's parody, would the same passage appear in a popular newspaper?

> Using your loaf won't fill your bread-bin, a mystery preacher warned in a pulpit blast yesterday.

> And punters will be pipped to know that though the horse they backed is first past the post – they won't pick up their winnings.

> HE-MEN have had it, according to the no-holds-barred sermon...

That's not style. But it's what gets into newspapers.

Out to Lunch...

Keith Waterhouse is very particular about what lunch is not: 'It is not prawn cocktail, steak and Black Forest gateau with your bank manger. It is not civic, commemorative, annual office or funeral. It is not when either party is on a diet, on the wagon or in a hurry.'

He is equally precise about what lunch is: 'It is a mid-day meal taken at leisure by, ideally, two people. Three's a crowd, four always split like a double amoeba into two pairs, six is a meeting, eight is a conference... A little light business may be touched upon but the occasion is firmly social. Whether they know it or not, for as long as they linger in the restaurant they are having an affair. The affair is lunch.'

The Theory and Practice of Lunch is an authoritative and delightfully witty manual on the art of taking the most agreeable meal of the day, written by a shrewd observer of the passing show who listed his sole hobby in *Who's Who* as 'Lunch'.

'Informative, sensible, well-written, entirely unpretentious... well worth the price of a bottle of house red' – *The Observer*.

'Part of its charm is that it has been written with so much obvious pleasure that the enjoyment seeps out of the pages.' – Roy Hattersely in *The Listener*.

'Relentless opinionated and very entertaining... irresistible.' – Kingsley Amis in *The Spectator*.

THE THEORY AND PRACTICE OF LUNCH

By Keith Waterhouse

Published by Revel Barker at £9.99

Revel Barker
Publishing

Publish and be Damned!
The astonishing story of the Daily Mirror

Cassandra: This book sparkles and flashes like a welder's arc. It has everything. Even the damned impudence to include disrespectful and distressing tales in the worst possible taste about myself.

The Observer: With its sensationalist approach, its chunks of sex, its comic strips and stripping comics, the *Daily Mirror* expresses the mood of the early fifties… The book is constructed like a series of spasms. Mr Cudlipp writes in *Daily Mirror* style. He beats the big drum but takes you round behind the scenes to watch the bearded lady shave.

Manchester Guardian: A highly entertaining book, full of the *Mirror* qualities of liveliness and audacity… The *Mirror* is an acquired taste and too often leaves a bad one behind. So does strong drink, which also a great many people seem to like.

The Spectator: Having backed the wrong horse in the abdication crisis, the *Mirror* then picked a winner with its anti-appeasement line. This brought clashes with *The Times.* Geraldine House accused Printing House Square of having a fifth column, of pursuing a policy 'that has put heart into every reader who has the Fascist and anti-democratic cause at heart.'

News Chronicle: …worth the study of the followers of any type or standards of journalism.

PUBLISH AND BE DAMNED!

By Hugh Cudlipp

Published by Revel Barker at £12.99

Revel Barker
Publishing

Lightning Source UK Ltd.
Milton Keynes UK
UKOW06f1942311017
311970UK00013B/875/P